TRACING Y
GREAT W
ANCESTORS

The Gallipoli Campaign

FAMILY HISTORY FROM PEN & SWORD

Tracing Your Army Ancestors
Simon Fowler

•

Tracing Your Pauper Ancestors
Robert Burlison

•

Tracing Your Yorkshire Ancestors
Rachel Bellerby

•

Tracing Your Air Force Ancestors
Phil Tomaselli

•

Tracing Your Northern Ancestors
Keith Gregson

•

Tracing Your Black Country Ancestors
Michael Pearson

•

Tracing Your Textile Ancestors
Vivien Teasdale

•

Tracing Your Railway Ancestors
Di Drummond

•

Tracing Secret Service Ancestors
Phil Tomaselli

•

Tracing Your Police Ancestors
Stephen Wade

•

Tracing Your Royal Marine Ancestors
Richard Brooks
and Matthew Little

•

Tracing Your Jewish Ancestors
Rosemary Wenzerul

•

Tracing Your East Anglian Ancestors
Gill Blanchard

•

Tracing Your Ancestors
Simon Fowler

•

Tracing Your Liverpool Ancestors
Mike Royden

•

Tracing Your Scottish Ancestors
Ian Maxwell

•

Tracing British Battalions on the Somme
Ray Westlake

•

Tracing Your Criminal Ancestors
Stephen Wade

•

Tracing Your Labour Movement Ancestors
Mark Crail

•

Tracing Your London Ancestors
Jonathan Oates

•

Tracing Your Shipbuilding Ancestors
Anthony Burton

•

Tracing Your Northern Irish Ancestors
Ian Maxwell

•

Tracing Your Service Women Ancestors
Mary Ingham

•

Tracing Your East End Ancestors
Jane Cox

•

Tracing the Rifle Volunteers
Ray Westlake

•

Tracing Your Legal Ancestors
Stephen Wade

•

Tracing Your Canal Ancestors
Sue Wilkes

•

Tracing Your Rural Ancestors
Jonathan Brown

•

Tracing Your House History
Gill Blanchard

•

Tracing Your Tank Ancestors
Janice Tait and David Fletcher

•

Tracing Your Family History on the Internet
Chris Paton

•

Tracing Your Medical Ancestors
Michelle Higgs

•

Tracing Your Second World War Ancestors
Phil Tomaselli

•

Tracing Your Channel Islands Ancestors
Marie-Louise Backhurst

•

Tracing Great War Ancestors DVD
Pen & Sword Digital &
Battlefield History TV Ltd

•

Tracing Your Prisoner of War Ancestors: The First World War
Sarah Paterson

•

Tracing Your British Indian Ancestors
Emma Jolly

•

Tracing Your Naval Ancestors
Simon Fowler

•

Tracing Your Huguenot Ancestors
Kathy Chater

•

Tracing Your Servant Ancestors
Michelle Higgs

•

Tracing Your Ancestors from 1066 to 1837
Jonathan Oates

•

Tracing Your Merchant Navy Ancestors
Simon Wills

•

Tracing Your Lancashire Ancestors
Sue Wilkes

•

Tracing Your Ancestors through Death Records
Celia Heritage

•

Tracing Your West Country Ancestors
Kirsty Gray

•

Tracing Your First World War Ancestors
Simon Fowler

•

Tracing Your Army Ancestors - 2nd Edition
Simon Fowler

•

Tracing Your Irish Family History on the Internet
Chris Paton

•

Tracing Your Aristocratic Ancestors
Anthony Adolph

•

Tracing Your Ancestors from 1066 to 1837
Jonathan Oates

•

TRACING YOUR GREAT WAR ANCESTORS

The Gallipoli Campaign

A Guide for Family Historians

Simon Fowler

Pen & Sword
FAMILY HISTORY

First published in Great Britain in 2015
PEN & SWORD FAMILY HISTORY
an imprint of
Pen & Sword Books Ltd
47 Church Street
Barnsley
South Yorkshire
S70 2AS

ISBN 978 1 47382 368 6

A CIP catalogue record for this book is
available from the British Library.

Typeset in Palatino and Optima by
CHIC GRAPHICS

Printed and bound in England by
CPI Group (UK), Croydon, CR0 4YY

Pen & Sword Books Ltd incorporates the imprints of Pen & Sword
Archaeology, Atlas, Aviation, Battleground, Discovery, Family History,
History, Maritime, Military, Naval, Politics, Railways, Select, Social History,
Transport, True Crime, Claymore Press, Frontline Books, Leo Cooper,
Praetorian Press, Remember When, Seaforth Publishing and Wharncliffe.

For a complete list of Pen & Sword titles please contact
PEN & SWORD BOOKS LTD
47 Church Street, Barnsley, South Yorkshire, S70 2AS, England
E-mail: enquiries@pen-and-sword.co.uk
Website: www.pen-and-sword.co.uk

CONTENTS

PREFACE

There is no other way to put it. Gallipoli was a disaster from beginning to end. On paper at least, the campaign should have been winnable, but in the event the only thing that went well was the final evacuation. The reasons why it was such a disaster have long been debated by historians, and include poor commanding officers, insufficient training and preparation, a lack of resources – ammunition, hospital beds and even water – and also a lack of will to succeed. There were also many missed opportunities and a lot of bad luck.

Overall, the campaign showed how the British and, to an extent, their French allies had failed to grasp the realities of modern warfare. The landings at Anzac Cove and V Beach on 25 April and the attempts to break out from Anzac in early August were undoubtedly heroic but, without adequate artillery fire to destroy Turkish positions, flexible leadership by junior officers and proper preparation, they proved extremely costly in lives and materiel and ultimately they failed. It took two more years of bitter losses on the Western Front before the Allied commanders worked out a way to win.

Whichever way you look at the campaign, the heroism and the fortitude of the Anzac and the Tommy on the ground, who endured dysentery, drought and disaster with remarkable fortitude and great humour, are undeniable. Conditions here were every bit as bad as anywhere on the Western Front, and sometimes even worse.

This short book is designed to help people researching the men and the units who fought at Gallipoli. It does not go into detail about the battles or the strategies of the commanders, as there are numerous books that do this to a greater or lesser

An Australian field gun battery taking a break. British plans were severely hampered by the lack of artillery to destroy Turkish positions.

degree. A list is given in the bibliography. Instead, this book is arranged by sections offering guidance on researching the service personnel, the units and the actions themselves. There is considerable overlap between the sections, so readers may need to study them all to obtain a full picture. In addition, there are sections concerning life in the trenches and offering guidance for tourists, describing the key cemeteries, museums and other important attractions.

If possible, readers should really visit the Dardanelles to see at first hand where the fighting took place. Here, perhaps even more than on the Western Front, the sacrifices made by the British, the Australians and all the other men on both sides can be better appreciated.

DARDANELLES OR GALLIPOLI?

The campaign at Gallipoli is sometimes referred to as the Dardanelles campaign. Although there is some overlap, 'Gallipoli' can be taken to refer to those events that took place on land, and 'Dardanelles' to the less well known events at sea. This is how I use these terms in this book. However, contemporary papers often refer only to the Dardanelles, so in searching for material you may need to look under both terms. A minor further complication is that the Allied forces were part of a Mediterranean Expeditionary Force (MEF), and occasionally records may be found under this heading. By end of 1915 the MEF had also become responsible for the Allied forces in Salonika and, later, around the Suez Canal. Initially Lord Kitchener, the Secretary of State for War, wanted the Mediterranean Expeditionary Force to be called the Constantinople Expeditionary Force, until Sir Ian Hamilton, the Force commander, pointed out that the name was too much of a give-away, noting in his diary 'I begged him to alter this to avert Fate's evil eye.'

The Turks describe the whole sorry farrago as the Battle of Çanakkale or the *Çanakkale Savaşi*.

Chapter 1

GALLIPOLI – AN OVERVIEW

From the start the campaign in Gallipoli was a mistake. It was launched in haste and with insufficient preparation: it took barely a month to plan and arrange the most ambitious amphibious landing in British history since the equally ill-fated Crimean Expedition of 1854. And the Turks were well very aware that an invasion was imminent. This meant that the Allied

An illustration from the Graphic *showing the Gallipoli peninsula as seen from the air. The ridged nature of the terrain is immediately apparent.*

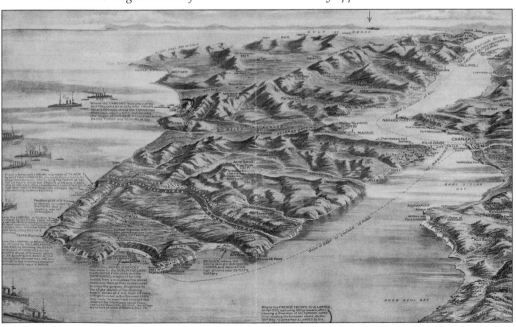

1

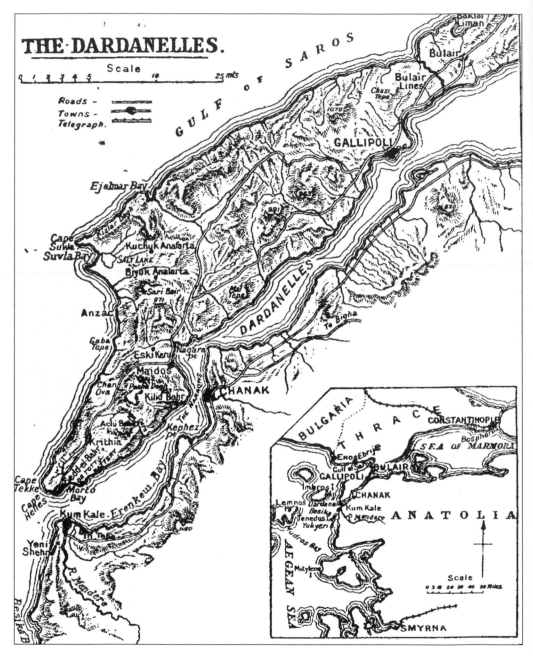

A relief map of the Gallipoli peninsula. The terrain heavily influenced the nature of the fighting.

commander, Sir Ian Hamilton, rarely had the advantage of surprise and formulated his plans on scant information. The latest maps available, for example, dated from the 1890s and gave no real idea of the lie of the land. Most information about the landing beaches came from observation by officers on board Royal Navy ships several miles away. Admiralty documents at The National Archives contain many drawings made by officers.

Equally importantly, in both London and Paris the campaign was treated as a sideshow and kept short of men and armaments. This was not helped by Hamilton's deferential and optimistic nature, which meant that he did not press hard enough for what was needed.

Sir Ian Standish Monteith Hamilton, then aged 62, had had a long and distinguished career in army service during the Boer War and in India. But he proved a disappointment in the realities of modern warfare, and the failings of the Gallipoli campaign can in large measure be placed on his shoulders. According to George H. Cassar's biography of Hamilton in the *Oxford Dictionary of National Biography*:

He had personal charm, integrity, more experience of war than any of his contemporaries, intellectual detachment, and physical courage. His flaws were not as visible but they proved fatal. He lacked mental toughness, basic common sense, and sufficient ruthlessness to dismiss an incompetent subordinate. He underestimated the enemy, a cardinal sin in war, and his excessive optimism frequently

General Sir Ian Hamilton, who led the Mediterranean Expeditionary Force for much of the campaign. There is still considerable debate about how effective he was as the force's commander.

crossed into the realm of wishful thinking. While it was theoretically sound to refrain from interfering in field operations once in progress, it was unwise to adhere to that principle when subordinates were unproven or inadequate. The plain truth was that throughout the Gallipoli campaign he never acted like a commander-in-chief.

In the end the only thing that went to plan was the evacuation in the early days of January 1916, which was brilliantly executed.

But why Gallipoli? Even at the time it seemed a puzzling choice. The reason lay hundreds of miles away on the Western Front, where the war had settled down to a bloody stalemate. The British were attracted by the idea that by opening another front the Germans would be forced to divert resources away from the Western Front.

At the start of 1915 Winston Churchill, the First Lord of the Admiralty, persuaded the Cabinet to send a fleet to force a passage through the Dardanelles with the object of compelling Turkey's surrender and thus helping beleaguered Serbia and Russia. Turkey had joined the war on Germany's side in November 1914. The War Office soon came under heavy political pressure to send troops to assist the fleet. Lord Kitchener, the British Minister of War, asked Hamilton to command the military force, explaining that the Admiralty was confident that its ships could get through the waterway unaided, in which case he thought it likely that Constantinople would surrender. He expected the army's role would be limited to landing parties to destroy any hidden guns that might impede progress to a successful occupation of Constantinople. But he made it clear that if the navy encountered unforeseen obstacles, Hamilton was to throw his full force into clearing the way. 'Having entered on the project of forcing the Straits,' Kitchener remarked, 'there can be no idea of abandoning the scheme.' Kitchener's parting words summed up the reasons for the operation: 'If the fleet gets through, Constantinople will fall of itself and you will have won not a battle, but the war.'

On paper the omens looked good. The Turkish army was not highly rated: it had recently been beaten in two short wars in the Balkans and had just lost a major battle against the Russians in Eastern Anatolia in January 1915. British troops in Egypt were told that: 'Turkish soldiers as a rule manifest their desire to surrender by holding their rifle butt upwards and by waving clothes or rags of any colour. An actual white flag should be regarded with the utmost suspicion as a Turkish soldier is unlikely to possess anything of that colour.' The fighting skills and resourcefulness of 'Johnnie Turk' would come as a shock.

Yet, taking the Dardanelles was still a challenge. The Straits are protected by the hilly Gallipoli peninsula to the north, and by the shores of Asia Minor to the south. In 1915 fortresses well positioned on the cliff-tops guarded the shipping lanes. As visitors to Gallipoli will testify, the peninsula itself is hardly an ideal place either to land on or to fight over. Beyond the narrow bays and escarpments at Cape Helles, where the Dardanelles meet the Aegean Sea, a low plain rises behind the seashore village of Sedd-el-Bahr and stretches north to the inland village of Krithia (now Alçitepe). Beyond it crouches Achi Baba, a deceptively unimposing hill with a broad-breasted summit just high enough to command a view of both the Aegean and the Dardanelles. Further north on the western coastline the land takes on a wilder aspect. Sheer cliffs scarred with deep gullies and ravines sweep down almost to the water's edge and tower up to rugged heights of formidable grandeur. Inland there are deep gullies (called nullahs by the British) – dried-up watercourses that become torrents after rain – and narrow razor-edged ridges. Much of the vegetation is thorny, impenetrable scrub, although to the British observers on naval ships in 1915 it had looked lush and green. Describing the hills northeast of Anzac Cove, the location

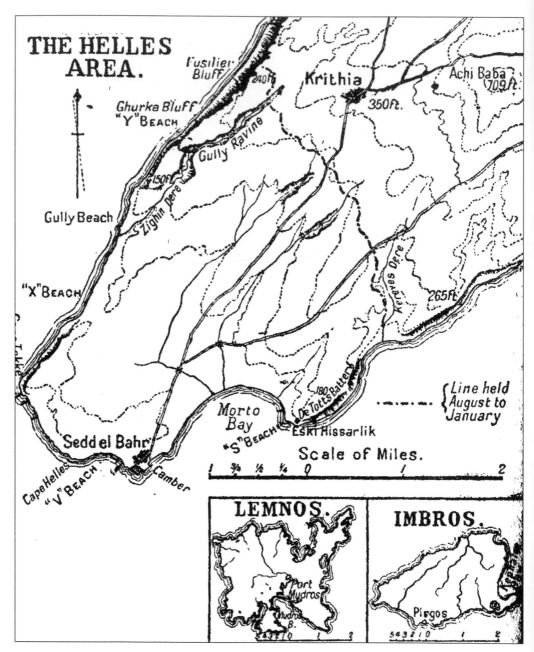

The area around Cape Helles at the tip of Gallipoli, showing the beaches where many of the landings took place on 25 April 1915.

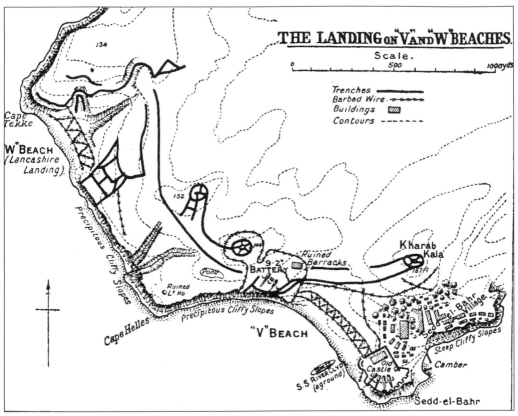

A larger-scale map showing V and W beaches and the positions in the days after the landings on 25 April.

of Australian, New Zealand and British attacks in early August, the British official history notes:

> No account of the operations . . . can hope to convey any adequate idea of the extreme difficulties of the undertaking if the reader does not first try to visualise the bewildering nature of the country through the troops were to march. The spurs and gullies are so contorted, so rugged and steep, and so thickly covered with dense prickly scrub, that their passage is difficult enough in peacetime . . . But in August 1915 the only available maps were very inadequate and

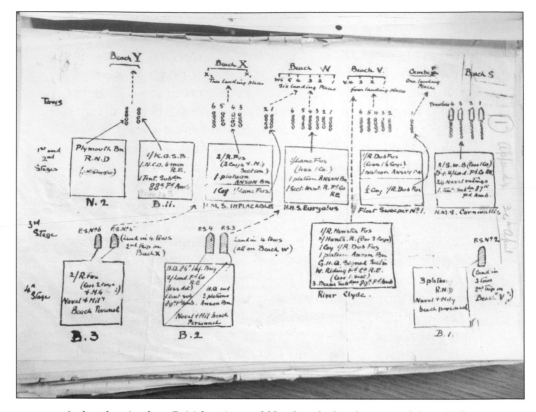

*A plan showing how British units would land on the beaches around Cape Helles.
(TNA WO 95/4311)*

those arduous routes had to be traversed at night by heavily
laden men who were harassed by an invisible enemy and
led by guides who themselves had very little real knowledge
of the ground.

During February and March several attempts were made by the
British and French navies to force the Straits. The first attack took
place on 19 February. Despite pounding the outer fortresses, poor
Allied gunnery meant that the British and French attack proved

ineffective in the face of an efficient Turkish defensive system, although more damage was done than the Allies realised. A renewed bombardment the following week was similarly unsuccessful. In particular, the Allied guns could not effectively silence the Turkish mobile batteries that poured down shellfire from the heights. Almost a month later, on 18 March, naval forces attempted to force their way through the 2-mile-wide Narrows between Gallipoli and Asia Minor, but had to abandon the attempt when three ships were lost in a previously unknown minefield. The disaster was observed by Hamilton, who concluded that the navy could not get through without the army's help.

Intensive preparations were made to land troops at Cape Helles on the tip of the peninsula, and further up as a diversionary feint. Vast numbers of ships were purchased in harbours across the Middle East and fresh troops arrived in Egypt, including men of the Australian and New Zealand Army Corps (ANZAC) who were actually on their way to France.

In the meantime the Turks naturally also made preparations. As a measure of the extent of German influence over Turkish policy, regional command was placed in the hands of General Liman von Sanders, the head of the German military mission in Constantinople. Liman sent German and Turkish troops to strategic locations around Gallipoli. The British observed the Turkish preparations. Tell-tale streaks of newly turned earth showed that they were digging trenches, and banks of new barbed wire caught the sun. After one reconnoitring trip, Hamilton ruefully wrote to Lord Kitchener that 'Gallipoli looks a much tougher nut to crack than it did over the map in your office'.

The first British troops landed on the peninsula just before dawn on 25 April 1915. The Allied Expeditionary Force consisted of eighty-four ships in total, carrying 75,056 men (including 30,638 Australians and New Zealanders under the command of

Turkish shells landing off W Beach a few days after the Allied landings.

General William Birdwood), together with the men of a French division, 16,481 horses and mules, and 3,104 vehicles.

The previous night the Royal Naval Division had mounted a diversionary attack at Bulair at the northern end of the peninsula; a flat area, and much closer to Constantinople, it looked like a natural place for any invasion to take place. Liman von Sanders was convinced that this was where the British would land in strength and it took a day for him to realise his mistake. It was, in the words of Lyn Macdonald, his 'first and only gaffe of the campaign'.

The main thrust of the attack focused on five beaches (named S, V, W, X and Y) along Helles Point and was carried out by men of the 29th Division, who were ferried from Royal Navy ships positioned a mile or so off the coast. Some two thousand men were killed during the first day. Further down the peninsula troops were streaming ashore on the beaches around Cape Helles. Here, at V Beach, the Turks were well dug in in the cliffs above the beach and only opened fire as the armada of small vessels carrying the British troops drew close to the beach. As the British landed, they were mown down by Turkish fire. Colonel Williams, who was supervising the landing, noted in his war diary: '9am. Very little directed fire against the ship, but fire immediately concentrates on any attempt to land. The Turk's fire discipline is really wonderful. Fear we will not land today.'

Turkish shells landing among British ships off Cape Helles.

11

Brigadier General Cecil Aspinall-Oglander, the official historian of the Gallipoli campaign, described the landing on V Beach:

> When the boats were only a few yards from the shore, Hell was suddenly let loose. A tornado of fire swept over the incoming boats, lashing the calm waters of the bay as with a thousand whips. Devastating casualties were suffered in the first few seconds. Some of the boats drifted helplessly away with every man in them killed. Many more of the Dubliners [Royal Dublin Fusiliers] were killed as they waded ashore. Other, badly wounded, stumbling in the waters, were drowned.

When almost a thousand casualties had been lost, it was agreed to call off the landing until nightfall. But for the relative weakness of the Turkish forces on the southern peninsula – where the landings at S and Y beaches were unopposed – the whole Allied operation might well have been thrown back into the sea.

Rear Admiral R.W. Wemyss, who was in command of the naval forces, described the landings at W Beach:

> . . . the fire, though not quite so murderous as on V Beach, was tremendous. In spite of this, all the boats landed, and the Lancashire Fusiliers jumped out of them only to meet what appears to be an almost impassable wire entanglement, in their attempts to pass which the leading men were nearly all killed.
>
> Watching this incident, as I was, from the fore bridge of the Euryalus, it seemed as though the impossible had been performed, for before many minutes had passed it became clear that the beach was gained. I cannot conceive that it has ever been the lot of anybody to witness a finer exhibition of dash and heroism. The boat's crews who

Lancashire Landing (W Beach), where men from the 1st Lancashire Fusiliers attempted to land in the early hours of 25 April. No fewer than six Victoria Crosses were awarded for acts of heroism during the landing.

showed equal spirit were much knocked about, but in all cases managed to get their boats back, although sometimes with not more than two men able to pull an oar.

Of the thousand Lancashire Fusiliers who landed, six hundred lost their lives.

The landings were supported by a dawn attack 15 miles to the north by men of the Australian and New Zealand Army Corps under General William Birdwood. The beach swiftly became known as Anzac Cove, or just Anzac. Unfortunately, the troops landed at the wrong beach, a swift current having carried them a mile north of their intended target. By the time this was realised, it was too late to go back. Captain Herbert Kenyon of the Royal Artillery was among the first wave of troops:

It was about eight or ten yards from the water's edge to the foot of the hills and we all doubled in under the bank and then we went after the others, shouting, yelling, cursing, tumbling down and tripping over bushes and holes. It was impossible for the men to climb in their kit so they chucked them as they scrambled up.

Soon the Turkish guns started firing on the beach and on the men who were either clambering up the cliff side or had already reached the top. Everywhere there was chaos. The Allied ships were unable to fire their guns against the Turkish positions for fear of hitting their own troops. During the day some nine hundred men lost their lives here.

After the landings, little was done by the British to exploit the situation and, apart from a few limited advances inland by small groups of men, most troops stayed on or close to the beaches. The attack lost momentum and the Turks had time to bring up reinforcements and rally the small number of defending troops.

Having established, at great cost, two beachheads at Anzac and Cape Helles, Hamilton determined to extend the Allied position in the south, with attacks directed towards the village of Krithia (now Alçitepe). Three successive operations were launched, all of which were thrown back by Liman's increasingly effective Turkish defence force. Ironically, a small number of British troops had actually entered the village on 25 April, but withdrew because they had no orders to take Krithia. Had they remained there, it is likely that the Gallipoli campaign would have been successful.

By 4 May it was clear that without troop reinforcements there was no hope of victory. Several months of intense trench warfare ensued. Such were the conditions on the peninsula that almost no location was safe from enemy bombardment or snipers. Artillery support was also ineffective. An early lesson from the Western Front had been the need for sufficient guns to pound enemy positions and demoralise their troops. At Gallipoli this only rarely happened, in part due to ammunition shortages. Lieutenant Colonel Grant of the Royal Artillery later grumbled that: 'It was a mistake to conquer the Turks with 8 Howitzers [heavy guns] and little ammunition.' The Royal Navy battleships possessed sufficiently powerful guns, but it was hard for their gunnery officers to pinpoint targets and there was the constant worry that they might end up shelling the Allied ground troops. On 9 May Brigadier Cunliffe-Owen, who was in charge of the Anzac artillery, wrote: 'it must be understood that naval guns cannot fire on enemy's guns close to our [Anzac] line. It is too dangerous because all fire from ships is by compass, as the map is not accurate . . .'.

Attempts to use aircraft to observe the effectiveness of artillery barrages were also frustrated, in part because very few planes were available, but a more serious problem was the lack of communication between the observers and the ships. Pilots complained that after they had flown to the right position and given the ready sign, there was a delay of an hour or two before the ship opened fire. Then the ship would either fire slowly or simply leave, generally to avoid counter-fire from the enemy. In addition, the aircraft often experienced mechanical difficulties and there was an acute shortage of air observers. A post-war report on Gallipoli concluded that: 'It is clearly proved that the fire of ship's guns cannot be considered an adequate substitute for well-organised support of field or heavy artillery on land.'

Back in London, the Cabinet was becoming increasingly desperate for accurate information about the situation in the Dardanelles. At the end of July Sir Maurice Hankey, Secretary to the government's Dardanelles Committee, was sent to investigate. Scrambling up Gully Ravine, he found that 'proper sanitation is impossible in places as the Turkish dead lie in heaps, the smell being bad, while the thought of masses of flies in such conditions makes the flesh creep'. One of the beaches was 'really rather horrible. A dust storm rages for a great part of most days, the sun is intensely hot, of shade there is none . . . the flies are execrable, and worst of all, the Turks shell at frequent intervals.' Hankey was, however, particularly impressed by the Anzacs:

> Their physique is wonderful and their intelligence in high order. Harassed by continuous shelling, living in intense heat . . . compelled to carry their water and most of their supplies and ammunition by hand 400 feet up the hills and deprived of any recreation except occasional bathing, they are nevertheless in the highest sprits and spoiling for a fight.

In fact, the Australians and New Zealanders were pretty fed up with the diet and with the monotony of everyday existence with no rest to look forward to. One man grumbled to Colonel George Beith, 24th Battalion AIF, that 'If I could get off this bloody place I'd volunteer to scrub out the Melbourne exhibition building with a toothbrush.'

The retrieval and burial of the dead lying out in no man's land between the two sets of trenches proved particularly difficult. Near Anzac a short armistice was held on 19 May for this purpose. Likewise, the war diary of the 2nd South Wales Borderers for the morning of 3 May noted that: 'Turkish burial parties under cover of a white flag searched the ground in front of the immediate front. We accordingly also sent out parties to bury the Turkish dead, of whom there was a great quantity just in front of our right flank.' [WO 95/4311]

On 6 August 1915 fresh British and French troops landed on A, B and C Beaches at Suvla Bay in an attempt to break the deadlock. Suvla Bay lay a dozen miles or so north from Helles on the Aegean side of the peninsula. On paper it seemed ideal, being flat and wide enough to allow British and French forces to disembark easily, and with few Turkish defences. The operation

The area around Anzac Cove and Suvla Bay on the west of the peninsula, where much of the fiercest fighting took place.

The view from a Royal Navy ship of the landings at Suvla Bay on 6 August 1915.

took the form of a three-pronged attack: a diversionary action at Helles, which was cut to shreds by Turkish artillery; a movement northwards from Anzac Cove towards Sari Bair, which lay halfway to Suvla; and the centrepiece of the offensive: a landing in force at Suvla by fresh divisions under General Sir Frederick Stopford. The idea was for Stopford's forces to link up with the troops at Anzac Cove and make a clean sweep across the Gallipoli peninsula.

The landings at Suvla Bay achieved total surprise and Stopford's initial progress was almost unopposed. However, the wider offensive rapidly lost momentum as the result of indecision by the commanders and their failure to press home the battle.

Stopford had been recalled out of retirement and had had no experience of commanding troops in battle. He also had deep doubts about the plan that had been agreed. And worst of all, he had little idea about what was going on because he changed his mind about moving his headquarters to Suvla and instead remained on board a ship stationed off the coast. His inactivity and complacency forced his removal in mid-August, but by then the damage had been done. According to Nigel Steel, author of *Gallipoli* (1999): 'Stopford did not believe in the possibility of success, and so did not drive his men to fulfil it. He allowed the failure in which he believed to come about'. Rather more succinctly, Wikipedia describes his performance in command as 'one of the most incompetent feats of generalship in the First World War'.

It probably did not help that the troops available for the landing hardly inspired confidence. The official historian, Brigadier Aspinall-Oglander, graphically described XI Corps as being like a motor car 'whose hurried assembly had only been completed by the inclusion of spare parts of various different makes . . . Doubtless before using it for important work Sir Ian Hamilton should have tested it. But he had no space [to do so]. . . . No sooner was the car set in motion than its inherent faults became apparent.' Hamilton later commented that the combination of 'old generals and new troops' was fatal.

Sir Maurice Hankey, who went ashore on 8 August, found that: 'A peaceful scene greeted us. Hardly any shells. No Turks. Very occasional musketry. Bathing parties around the shore. There really seemed to be no realisation of the overwhelming necessities for a rapid offence, of the tremendous issues depending on the next few hours . . .'. Meanwhile the Anzacs were being torn apart as they attempted to break out of Anzac Cove to meet up with IX Corps, in accordance with the original plan. Turkish machine gun fire cut swathes through the Australians and New Zealanders who attempted to cross the pinnacles of Sari Bair and

Rhododendron Ridge. From the tops of these hills the troops could see Suvla Bay.

British troops too were soon in the thick of the action. At 6pm on 8 August Sir Ian Hamilton finally arrived at Suvla. He was appalled by the lethargy he found and immediately ordered an attack on a range of hills a few miles to the east of the bay, in the hope that success would lead to a British breakout into the flatter country beyond. However, the two days' delay since the landings had allowed the Turks to move their forces from the north and by the time the British assault on the hills began at dawn on the 9th, the Turks were streaming down to meet them.

Among the British forces was the 6th Battalion, East Yorkshire Regiment. Part of the New Army, which had been raised in the autumn of 1914 from the flood of volunteers to the colours, it had been designated the regiment's pioneer battalion, responsible for digging trenches, making repairs and building roads, and although the men had had some military training it was not expected that the battalion would see action. But due to the very heavy casualties in other units, it was decided to use the 6th Battalion as a normal infantry battalion, despite its inexperience. On the morning of the 9th the East Yorkshires began to clamber up Tekke Tepe hill. Confusion resulted in Lieutenant Colonel Henry Moore, the battalion's commanding officer, taking one company forward and leaving the three other companies to follow on as soon as they could be put in order. The first party initially took the hill, but all of them were then killed or captured (eyewitnesses reported that Moore himself was bayoneted by a Turkish soldier). The other companies attempted to advance but came under withering fire and were forced to retire. For that day the battalion's casualties were given as 13 officers killed, wounded or missing, 78 men killed and another 104 wounded. The failure of the British to take the hills meant that the Allies' last possible strategic move had been thwarted.

A few weeks later, on 21 August, the 6th Battalion, now some

12 officers and about 500 men strong, joined an attack on 'W' Hills, part of the Battle of Scimitar Hill, which developed into the largest land battle of the campaign. At 3pm, under cover of a naval barrage, two battalions went into the attack. The 6th Battalion was in support, but its men soon found themselves in action. Advancing, they took several Turkish trenches. Once they had achieved their objective, their orders were to wait to allow reinforcements to pass through their position to make a further advance. The battalion remained in position under heavy fire all day and into the night but no reinforcements came and by the next morning the men were exhausted, and running out of food, water and ammunition, Inevitably, their position was soon overrun by the Turks. What was left of the battalion retired to its original position. During this action the battalion lost 8 officers killed or wounded, and 22 men killed, 128 wounded and 49 missing.

The 6th Battalion had arrived at Suvla Bay with 26 officers and about 800 men. By the end of August no fewer than 21 officers and 198 men had been killed – a quarter of the battalion's strength.

As autumn arrived, the campaign ground to a halt and settled into an uncomfortable form of trench warfare. This was a disastrous state of affairs for the Allied forces. Momentum slowly drained away from the campaign as an uneasy stalemate emerged. Inevitably there was a general sense of frustration. According to Major H.C.B. Wemyss of the Royal Signals:

Extreme heat with dust and flies, very limited fresh water and no cover reduced men's stamina, while icy blizzards later on discovered any weaknesses. Variations in shelling and sniping made one day differ from another. No rest areas existed. No houses, no canteens, no leave or any prospect of it, and irregular mails from home – so time rolled on. [CAB 45/230]

Heavy rain in the autumn followed by snow turned the once dry-as-dust trenches into muddy quagmires, and conditions for the men deteriorated yet further. Clem Attlee, a company commander in the South Lancashires, bullied his men into staying alive by insisting on regular exercise and 'fairly frequent issues of rum', while dysentery, frostbite and drowning decimated the other companies in the battalion.

Confidence in the operation was dwindling, particularly as the French were reluctant to divert attention away from the battles in France. It did not help that the British and French were planning to support their Serbian allies by landing in Salonika. To Hamilton's great dismay, some troops were diverted away from Gallipoli and sent to Salonika. As it was, Hamilton was already facing increasing criticism from London as grim news of the expedition reached home, along with complaints of his mismanagement of the campaign.

London and Paris began to suggest that the Allied forces should be evacuated. Hamilton retaliated by estimating that casualties in any such evacuation would run at up to 50 per cent: a startlingly high figure. On 11 October Hamilton was summoned to London to appear before the politicians and military men of the Dardanelles Committee; he never returned to Gallipoli.

Hamilton was replaced by Sir Charles Monro, who had previously commanded the Third Army on the Western Front. He was asked by Lord Kitchener 'to report fully and frankly on the military situation'. Monro consulted his divisional commanders, who were unanimous that their men were in no fit state to take the offensive. Indeed, they feared they would not be able to survive a sustained Turkish onslaught, in part because most of the men were too weak physically to put up much of a fight. Monro thus recommended evacuation as soon as was practicable. Winston Churchill, however, later viewed Monro's achievement with a somewhat jaundiced eye: 'he came, he saw, he capitulated', he wrote. However, Monro was proved to be right and Churchill wrong.

In London, only Kitchener remained unpersuaded, and decided to see the situation for himself. Braving the winter storms, he arrived at Gallipoli on 10 November. Once ashore, Kitchener did not take long to make up his mind. Standing with General Birdwood at a post high above Anzac, he put his hand on the general's arm and said: 'Thank God, Birdie, I came to see this for myself. You were quite right. I had no idea of the difficulties you were up against.' Accepting the inevitable, he recommended evacuation on 15 November, overriding suggestions by the navy that they be allowed to attempt another naval assault.

It took the War Cabinet until 7 December to finally commit to evacuation. But by then the Allied troops were severely affected by the winter weather. On 12 November a severe storm had flooded many dug-outs and washed away stores, and previously dry watercourses became raging torrents, drowning many men. Hundreds more died of exposure. The troops at Suvla were worst affected as there was little shelter. For their part the Turks were equally hit by the storm.

The rain could be torrential. The weekly report of the Royal Naval Division for 21 December commented:

A thunderstorm and heavy rain last night did more damage than a month's shelling. In many places trenches and communicating trenches are impassable and everywhere mud renders movement slow and difficult. This has seriously interfered with works in progress, every spare man being required to assist in drainage and necessary repairs. [ADM 137/3086]

Fortunately when the evacuation began, there was a long spell of fine weather. Some 83,000 men and 186 guns, plus stores, were

Men waiting at Suvla to be evacuated. The evacuation in December and January was undoubtedly the most successful part of the whole sorry story, with only three men lost.

ANZAC troops engaged in a training exercise. Contemporary captions said that the men were going over the top to charge a Turkish position just before the evacuation, but the men's dress and demeanour suggest this was not the case.

successfully taken off from Anzac Cove and Suvla Bay between 10 and 20 December. The evacuation from Helles took place a few days later, between 28 December and 9 January 1916.

The evacuation operation was easily the most successful element of the entire campaign, with the loss of just three men. Painstaking efforts had been made to deceive the Turks into believing that the movements of the Allied forces did not constitute a withdrawal. However, there is some evidence to suggest that the Turks knew perfectly well what was happening but were content for the evacuation to take place because their troops were in almost as bad a condition.

The Deputy Quartermaster General Walter Campbell summarised the difficulties:

> A retirement in the face of an enemy on land where you have plenty of room is a very difficult and critical operation but under the circumstances here, where one is bang up against your enemy, and where you have absolutely no room to swing a cat, and also have to embark in small craft every single man, gun, animals and stores on a beach which is under the enemy's gunfire, and of which they know the range to the inch . . . you can imagine what a difficult anxious job it is. We have not only the enemy to contend with, but at any moment . . . a south-west wind might blow up.

The stores and kit which remained behind were either destroyed or booby-trapped. According to Company Sergeant Major William Burrows of the Anzacs:

> Before the last of us left, all the available ammunition and bombs were collected. These were buried and on a cross stuck into the ground was the following inscription 'To the Memory of Private Bullet RIP'. That was to prevent the Turks

from becoming inquisitive and digging up the ammunition and the bombs.

Various stratagems were used to conceal the withdrawal from the Turks. Ingenious devices to fire guns automatically were devised, while the men's feet were muffled to deaden the noise as they left their trenches, and on the beaches they maintained strict silence while waiting to be taken off. Sapper Eric Wattern was one of the last to leave:

> The last day was rather queer. One would feel very much the same sensation on being left behind alone in a house that had been one's home after the family and the furniture had gone. Two French 75s near our camp were very successfully trying to pretend that they were a battery of four guns . . . Ate as much as we could possibly tackle, to use up the surplus grub, and spent a happy evening opening bully and jam tins and chucking them down a well, also biffing holes in dixies and generally mucking up any serviceable articles.

After a period of rest the best troops, notably the Royal Naval battalions and the Anzacs, were sent to the Western Front, where they distinguished themselves in very different conditions on the Somme. The others spent the rest of the war in Palestine, Mesopotamia and Salonika.

It is hard to believe that anything good came from the landings in Gallipoli and the resulting eight months of misery. A number of authors have argued that the campaign could have been successful had sufficient resources been available. The future British Prime Minister Clement Attlee, who served as a junior officer at Gallipoli, believed its failure was due to the myopic concentration by the Allied High Command on the Western Front. And the Australian official historian Charles Bean made

A French .75 gun in action near Cape Helles. The French supplied both ships and large numbers of troops, but their contribution is often overlooked by historians.

this telling point in the conclusion to his account of the involvement of the Anzacs at Gallipoli: 'The real stake – the opening of communication with Russia, the crushing of Turkey, and the securing of allies in the Balkans – was worth playing for, providing that it was attainable by the means employed; but nothing could justify the initiation of the enterprise by means which could not attain the goal.'

But there were more problems than just a lack of resources. The British commanders were unimaginative and cautious, and did not make the best use of the resources available to them. Peter Hart points to the woeful operational planning and the inability to take advantage of any local tactical advantages:

> This endemic military incompetence at command and staff level was then lethally combined with troops that had little or no experience of modern warfare in 1915. The lesson was clear: raw courage was not enough to combat bolt-action rifles, machine guns, trench systems, barbed wire and above all artillery. Amateurism was doomed and the British Army needed a more professional approach if it was to triumph in the Great War.

In all, some 56,707 British, Australian and French men lost their lives, and another 124,000 were wounded. But lessons were learnt about seaborne landings that would ultimately prove invaluable thirty years later on D-Day.

In particular, the Australians and New Zealanders proved themselves as a fighting force second to none, leading to an increased sense of national pride. The miserable performance of their British commanders began to sow doubts in the minds of politicians and their electorates back home that led to increasing demands for their governments to have a bigger say in the direction of the war.

The Allies had the great advantage of surprise, initially on 25 April and then at Suvla Bay in early August, but it was an advantage that was soon squandered. On the other hand, the Turks had good defensive positions and benefited from short supply lines. By September, however, a stalemate had arisen that was as deeply entrenched as that on the Western Front. Neither side had the resources to defeat the other. So for the commanders-in-chief in London, Paris and Berlin, Gallipoli soon became just another 'sideshow' using up precious resources for no real benefit.

ANZAC LANDING

Ellis Ashmead-Bartlett was one of the few war correspondents who covered Gallipoli. His dispatches praised the prowess and bravery of the troops, particularly the Anzacs, but he became more and more critical of their leadership and what he believed was the futile sacrifice of so many men. Having come ashore in Gallipoli, he was almost immediately arrested as a spy and was detained for a short period while his credentials were checked.

APRIL 24th. Throughout the morning there were scenes of unwonted activity in Mudros Bay. The warships changed their anchorage and took up fresh stations, and the crowded transports slowly made their way to the entrance of the harbour. At 3 p.m. our boats brought the 500 men of the 11th Australian Infantry on board for the last time. Numbered squares had been painted in white on the quarter-deck, and on each of these a company fell in. The men were then dismissed and made their way forward to the mess decks. The hospitable British tars handed over their limited accommodation to the newcomers, who were to bear the brunt of the attack. At 5 p.m., our force, the Second Division of the fleet, consisting of the *Queen* [Elizabeth], *Prince of Wales*, *London*, and *Majestic*, with four transports bearing troops, and the covering ships *Triumph, Bacchante,* and *Prince George,* slowly steamed out of the bay. As we passed through the long lines of waiting transports, our bands played the national anthems of all the Allies, and deafening cheers greeted our departure. It was the most majestic and inspiring spectacle I have ever seen, but withal there was an atmosphere of tragedy, of life and hope and joy, a sense that we will never see another sun sink to rest.

The weather was beautifully fine, and when we had cleared the entrance of the bay we turned our backs on Gallipoli and steamed due west to pass round the far side of the island of Lemnos, en route for a secret rendezvous only known to the Admiral. It is painfully obvious that we can only effect a local surprise, because the Turks, in Sir Ian Hamilton's own words, knew of the exact composition of his force before he ever left Egypt, and now they must have learnt from their aviators and spies, scattered amongst the islands, that our preparations are complete. They can also calculate on our striking between the waning of the old moon and the rising of the new.

At six o'clock the Australian contingent fell in on one

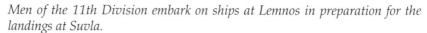

Men of the 11th Division embark on ships at Lemnos in preparation for the landings at Suvla.

side of the quarter-deck, and the crew of the *London* on the other. Captain Armstrong read Admiral de Robeck's proclamation wishing success to all ranks. His place was then taken by the ship's chaplain, who conducted a short service, and, as he uttered solemn prayers for victory, the men stood with bowed and bared heads. The Australians were then taken to the mess deck, where a hot meal was served out to them by the crew; then, after a smoke, they turned in to obtain some rest before dawn.

It was the last sleep for many a brave warrior from 'Down Under'.

At seven o'clock dinner was served in the wardroom, where the Australian officers were entertained as our guests. Everyone feigned an unnatural cheerfulness, the wine passed round, not a word was said of what the morrow might bring forth, yet over the party there seemed to hover the dread angel of death; after this tragic repast we surrendered our cabins to our Dominion friends, and snatched some sleep in the wardroom chairs. At sunset all lights were extinguished, and we steamed slowly through the night to an unknown destination, and to an unknown fate.

APRIL 25th. At 1 a.m. the fleet came to a dead stop and all on board were roused. I visited the mess decks, and watched the Australian troops having a final hot meal before falling in. They were as calm as if about to take part in a route march. At 2 a.m. the men fell in by companies on the numbered squares, of which I have already spoken. Boats had meanwhile been lowered and attached to the steam trawler which had towed three extra pinnaces from Mudros in addition to her own.

There was only a faint sheen from the stars to light up the dramatic scene on deck. This splendid contingent from

Australia stood there in silence, as the officers, hurrying from group to group, issued their final instructions. Between the companies of infantry were the beach parties, whose duty it was to put them ashore. Lieutenants in khaki, midshipmen – not yet out of their 'teens – in old white duck suits dyed khaki colour, carrying revolvers, water-bottles, and kits almost as big as themselves, and sturdy bluejackets equipped for the shore. At 2.30 a.m. the pinnace towed the boats alongside, and the Australians climbed down the wooden ladders. Thanks to the constant rehearsals there was no confusion, no overcrowding, and not a single mishap occurred. The tows then went astern, each battleship trailing four behind her. At 3 a.m., the fleet began to move slowly towards the shore until, a little after 4 a.m., the distant silhouette of the coast became visible for the first time. At 4.30 a.m. the *Queen, London, Prince of Wales*, and *Majestic* were in line about three thousand yards from the shore. The signal was then given for the tows to cast off, and make their way to the beach. It was still very dark and each pinnace, towing four boats, looked like a great snake as it slowly forged ahead.

We, who assembled on the bridge of the *London*, were now to pass some nerve-racking minutes of suspense which seemed like hours. Very slowly the twelve snakes of boats steamed past the battleships, the gunwales almost flush with the water, so crowded were they with khaki figures. To our anxious eyes it appeared as if the loads were too heavy for the pinnaces, that some mysterious power was holding them back, that they would never reach the shore before daybreak, and thus lose the chance of a surprise. The distance between the battleships and the boats did not diminish, but only because we were steaming very slowly in after them, until the water gradually shallowed.

Every eye and every glass was fixed on the grim line of hills in our front, so shapeless, yet so menacing in the gloom, the mysteries of which those in the boats, looking so fragile and helpless, were about to solve. Not a sound was heard from the shore and no light was seen; it appeared as if the enemy had been completely surprised, and that the Australians would land without opposition. The stars above the silhouette of the hills were frequently mistaken for lights. On the bridge a sharp-eyed signalman suddenly called out 'there's a light on the starboard bow', but after a brief examination it was pronounced to be a star, and this nautical astronomer turned away in confusion.

The progress of the boats was indeed slow, dawn was now breaking, and we feared they would never be able to land in the darkness. At last something definite did happen. Precisely at 4.50 a.m. the enemy showed an alarm signal, which flashed for ten minutes and then faded away. The next three minutes passed in breathless anxiety, for we could only just discern the outline of the tows, which appeared on the beach. At this moment seven destroyers conveying the rest of the covering troops glided through the intervals between the battleships and followed the boats inshore.

At 4.53 a.m. there came a very sharp burst of rifle fire from the beach, and we knew that our men were at last at grips with the enemy. The sound came as a relief, for the suspense of the prolonged waiting had become intolerable. The fire only lasted for a few minutes, and then a faint cheer was wafted across the water. How comforting and inspiring was the sound at such a moment! It came as a message of hope, for its meaning was clear: a foothold had been obtained on the beach.

At 5.23 a.m. the fire intensified, and we could tell from the sound that our men were in action. It lasted until 5.28

and then died down somewhat. It was impossible to see what was happening, although dawn was breaking, because we were looking due east into the sun, slowly rising behind the hills, and there was also a haze over the sea.

Throughout the afternoon the fighting continued, and the *London* was continually receiving signals to bombard positions, where the Turks were vigorously pressing the Australians back to the first line of hills they had seized at dawn. It became more and more obvious that the Dominion troops were extremely hard pressed. The wounded were brought off the shore in boats and pinnaces, in a never-ending stream, and the accommodation on the single hospital ship, allotted to Anzac, speedily gave out.

As usual, with the start of all British expeditions, the medical arrangements were totally inadequate to meet the requirements of the hour. Optimism had minimised our casualties to the finest possible margin, but the Turks multiplied them at an alarming rate. Apparently there was no one in authority to direct the streams of wounded to other ships where accommodation could be found for them, and many were taken on board the warships. Finally, orders came that the wounded were to be sent on board those transports which had already discharged their landing parties, and doctors would be sent aboard to look after them until they reached safety; many succumbed who might otherwise have been saved.

The boats returning to the *London* all brought the same tale of things going badly, heavy casualties, the beaches choked with wounded, who could not be moved, while the enemy's attack showed no diminution in strength or persistency. About 9.30 p.m., one of our pinnaces came off for fuel and water, and I was able to return in her to the beach. We steamed in close to the shore under what appeared to be a kind of hailstorm caused by the bullets striking the sea. Fortunately most of this fire was high, and I found some cover under the shelter of the hills, when I had landed on the narrow beach, some thirty yards wide. I climbed ashore over some barges in the semi-darkness amidst a scene of indescribable confusion. The beach was piled with ammunition and stores, hastily dumped from the lighters, among which lay the dead and wounded, and men so absolutely exhausted that they had fallen asleep in spite of the deafening noise of the battle. In fact, it was impossible to distinguish between the living and the dead in the darkness. Through the gloom I saw the ghost-like silhouettes of groups of men wandering around in a continuous stream apparently going to, or returning from, the firing-line.

On the hills above there raged an unceasing struggle lit up by the bursting shells, and the night air was humming with bullets like the droning of countless bees on a hot summer's day. Nevertheless, this little stretch of beach was so angled that it provided a haven of refuge – if a precarious one.

Ellis Ashmead-Bartlett, *Uncensored Dardanelles* (Hutchinson, 1928)

Chapter 2

SOLDIERS' LIVES

Conditions on Gallipoli were never good. In part this was due to the fact that everything had to be imported from Egypt or even from Britain. Even the water that was so vital in the hot summer months had to arrive by sea. Matters were not improved by the poor sanitary conditions, which inevitably led to debilitating outbreaks of dysentery and other diseases such as typhoid.

Supplying the Troops

All supplies came in by ship to one of the bays. Initially, supply ships were moored off the coast, but the threat of German submarine attacks from May onwards meant they had to unload everything in Lemnos – 60 miles away – and then small vessels would ferry it all to the coast. Tens of thousands of items, including food rations, other supplies and munitions, arrived each day. And once it had arrived on the beaches, it all had to be physically moved by hand or by cart to where it was needed. On a visit to Anzac, Sir Ian Hamilton found men 'staggering under huge sides of frozen beef; [and] men struggling up cliffs with kerosene tins full of water'.

With great difficulty depots were established at Helles and then at Suvla. Indeed, by the winter they were so well stocked that they had enough reserves to last the troops at least a month in case of emergency. Harold Thomas of the Army Medical Corps described Suvla in his memoirs:

An aerial oblique photograph of the Suvla Beach area showing the hospitals and stores areas which were constructed in the weeks after the landings.

Besides the hospital tents perhaps the most striking features of the landscape were the enormous dumps of ammunition and 'rations' – mountains of bully beef, and biscuits towered up foursquare to the sky; nearby were 'dumps ' for kinds of stores, one pathetic pile being formed of dead men's kit, haversacks, water-bottles, broken rifles, and all the flotsam and jetsam of the battlefield.

Even so, some things remained in short supply. In particular, it was hard to find wood for use in fires. Major B.G. Weller wrote:

Wood was so scarce that it was with the utmost difficulty men could collect enough scraps to make a small fire to boil water for their issue of tea. This led to a curious fact. It was noticed that men on the peninsula invariably walked with their eyes glued to the ground. The reason was soon apparent. They formed a habit of always looking for any scrap of wood or anything that would burn. Used matches even, were eagerly picked up and stored. [WO 95/4291]

FOOD AND DRINK

Food was plentiful if monotonous, but water was often in very limited supply. This is a constituent complaint found in memoirs and in oral history interviews with survivors. Even after sixty years Lieutenant R. Laidlaw remained critical of the arrangements made to support the troops during the Battle for Gully Ravine – a 2-mile-long dry valley on the western side of Gallipoli – on 28 June:

> We had plenty of ammunition, brought up earlier . . . but most of the men had drunk their water during the strenuous day and were now very thirsty – and thirst is not a pleasant thing, especially when you are serving in a sandy and hot country. All along the trench I could hear cries of 'water, water' and water there was none . . . There was none even for the wounded men and somehow I failed to get any message through to the destroyers when their boat came ashore to pick up the wounded.

DISEASE AND SANITATION

After Turkish bullets, the most serious killer of men was the tiny microbe that causes dysentery. The disease occurs when sanitation is poor, as was the case at Gallipoli. Even as recently as the Boer War it had been a major killer of soldiers, but it was

A major problem was the lack of fresh water for the troops. Here two water carriers bring precious supplies through a support trench.

not a serious problem on the Western Front, where strict measures were taken to ensure good sanitation in the trenches and proper care for those unfortunates who contracted the disease.

The authorities were well aware of the need for latrine discipline, but Gallipoli was a battlefield where every inch was fought over, so there was not the space, let alone the disinfectants, to provide proper sanitation. Even toilet paper was in short supply.

Little effort was made to control dysentery. The priority for medical aid was those wounded in battle. As well as the appalling latrines (where the disease bred), the food was poor. Clement Attlee drily commented in his memoirs that dysentery was 'a complaint for which our diet of bully beef, biscuit and tea without milk was not very suitable'. At the end of July Captain Attlee himself contracted dysentery: he was carried unconscious to the beach and sent to Malta to recover.

Sergeant H. Keighley of the Royal Artillery commented that dysentery

> was the biggest scourge we had on Gallipoli . . . I got dysentery very badly. I hadn't the strength to go up and down the cliff, across the ravine and up the hill to get to the Medical Officer (he was on the other side) and in the end I lost two or three stones. It was dreadful! I practically had to sleep alongside the latrines, my tummy had so much trouble.

Some men were affected so severely that they fouled themselves, thus undermining the sense of self-worth that is vital to good morale.

Another scourge that veterans remembered to their dying days was the flies, which initially emerged from the putrefying corpses in no man's land to make men's lives a living hell. Gunner

Dudley Menaud-Lissenburg of the Royal Field Artillery wrote that:

> We were invaded by millions of flies. There was no escape from these beastly insects. They swarmed around everywhere. Drinking and eating was a real nightmare and I avoided no matter how hungry I was the rice pudding, which was served up frequently mixed with currants and dehydrated fruit. It was difficult to distinguish currants from flies. They looked alike in this repulsive mixture. Immediately the lid was taken off the dixie the flies would swarm down and settle on the rim in a cluster and many of them would fall into the pudding . . . The ceilings of our bivouacs, a waterproof sheet, was black with flies crawling over each other and falling on top of one as you tried to rest.

In addition, dead soldiers became a real problem. There were several unofficial truces to allow each side to gather bodies from between the two front lines in no man's land. But in particularly hard-fought battles this was not always possible. At Hill 60 Francis Twistleton of the Otago Mounted Rifles found that in the trench in which he was stationed 'in many places the parapet and parados . . . was made up of dead men. Turks of course: the stench was appalling. I felt as though I could scrape the smell of the dead men out of my mouth and throat and stomach in chunks.' He was forced to report sick, although he was not actually sick, because he could keep no food down: 'I seemed to live on the smell of dead men and it was a very hard week.'

Less of a problem but still deeply unpleasant were the infestations of lice, which lived in the uniforms. On the Western Front there were delousing centres, which killed the lice, but there was no equivalent in the Dardanelles, so men spent hour after hour trying to kill the lice and the eggs they laid.

By October the health of the men had reached such a low point that their commanders were seriously worried that they would be unable to effectively repel any Turkish attacks, let alone mount any further offensive operations. As Peter Hart noted, 'the strength of the army was literally being leached away'. It was perhaps fortunate then that conditions in the enemy's lines were almost as bad.

REST AND RECREATION

Perhaps surprisingly, it was not all bad. In common with soldiers through the ages, the men tried to make the best of their circumstances. In the midst of the torrential rains of late October, Private Ernest Lye described his section:

> By rights I suppose we should have all been miserable, for we were wet through and very cold. The younger ones talked of the feeds they were going to have (I had a craving for hot muffins with piles of steaming butter), while the older ones talked of the pints they would drink when they got back to their favourite pub. Someone started a song which was taken up by all of us, until you would have thought we hadn't care in the world.

During the summer a favourite pastime was to cool off in the sea, although even here there was the chance of being hit by a stray Turkish shell. Most men thought it worth the risk to feel clean again.

SCIMITAR HILL

On 21 August the war journalist Ellis Ashmead-Bartlett observed the doomed British attack on Scimitar Hill. This was the last major battle on the peninsula. By now Ashmead-Bartlett was bitterly disillusioned with how the campaign had been conducted.

Suddenly at 3.15pm the bombardment switched off the enemy's lines and passed on to his artillery positions and communications. South-east of Chocolate Hill I saw long lines of our infantry (the 34th Brigade of the 11th Division) advance to the attack of the Turkish lines in the Biyuk Anafarta valley. Immediately the machine guns on Chocolate Hill concentrated on the parapets of the enemy's trenches to keep his infantry under cover. But the range was rather long and I do not think the Turks suffered much. In fact, when the 34th Brigade went forward I could see the Turkish soldiers standing fully exposed above the top of their sand-bags to fire on our lines. The 34th did capture one trench, but this seemed to be the extent of the success gained in this quarter. The 32nd and 33rd Brigades of the 11th Division should have supported this attack, but immediately after the start the line seemed to converge towards Hill 'W', on the lower spurs of which masses of our men remained throughout the afternoon, apparently quite unable to advance further. Here they were exposed to a withering fire from the trenches on Hill 'W', and also from those in the plain. I could follow the movements of small numbers of troops rushing forward only to be shot down and this disorganised mixture of battalions never regained any cohesion, and suffered many casualties.

The advance of our infantry caused the Turkish artillery to switch off most of their guns from Chocolate Hill to this new target, and it was possible to obtain a better view of what was passing. Sometime after 3.30 my attention was attracted by a sudden rush of our infantry (the 87th Brigade of the 29th Division, 2nd South Wales Borderers, 1st K.O.S.B.s [King's Own Scottish Borderers], 1st Inniskilling Fusiliers, and 1st Border Regiment) up the north-west slope of Scimitar Hill. Rushing with incredible speed through the

A sap at the top of Shrapnel Valley. The valley was the main route up from the beach area to the Anzac front line on the ridge.

smouldering scrub, this mass of khaki figures reached the bare sand-covered glacis near the top, charged right over it regardless of shells and bullets, and disappeared into the trenches.

From Chocolate Hill it looked as if the hill had been won, but only for a few minutes. Suddenly the Turkish artillery swept the crest of Scimitar Hill with shrapnel, the shells bursting incessantly, until a white canopy enveloped the summit. I watched some of our infantry chase the Turks down the reverse slope, but they were either killed or forced to retire from the fire from another trench or redoubt beyond, the existence of which was unsuspected. The tremendous concentration of shrapnel was too much for the shattered battalions. Soon I perceived khaki figures leaping from the trenches and dashing for cover to the scrub from which they had just emerged. The whole bare surface of the glacis remained dotted with our dead and wounded.

Meanwhile, another attack suddenly developed up the south-west slope of Scimitar Hill. (It was the 86th Brigade of the 29th Division, Royal Fusiliers, 1st Munster Fusiliers, 1st Lancashire Fusiliers, and 1st Dublin Fusiliers). These battalions, on leaving the trenches and entering the bush, found themselves intermingled with the men of the 11th Division, who should have advanced against the Turkish trenches in the Biyuk Anafarta valley more to the right, but they had gradually edged off to the left to obtain cover from the fire from the Turks in the valley, and were now in scattered groups all round Scimitar Hill.

When the leading battalion of the 86th Brigade attempted to continue its advance, it was apparently joined by many men of the 11th Division. I saw a dense mass of infantry, in no sort of formation, surging slowly up the south-west slope of Scimitar Hill. The confusion was awful, and, to add to it, at this moment the scrub began to blaze again. The disorganised soldiers vanished amidst the dense clouds of smoke and flame, and shortly afterwards reappeared on the bare, yellow glacis. Once again the Turkish artillery opened up with salvoes of shrapnel. The mass wavered, then broke, and men streamed back down the hill, leaving the summit still more thickly strewn with dead and dying. I watched the wounded endeavouring to crawl back to cover, if they did reach the scrub, they perished in the flames.

In fact, Scimitar Hill was now fairly ablaze. The attack had failed lamentably, but was not yet over . . .

The only reinforcement which had reached the

Peninsula since August 6th was the 2nd Mounted Division under General Peyton, which had arrived from Egypt without their horses. It was, throughout the afternoon, held in reserve behind Lala Baba and now, when the attack of the 29th Division had finally failed, de Lisle decided to throw it into the conflict.

It was sometime after 4.30 p.m. when my attention was suddenly attracted by the Turkish gunners lengthening their range and concentrating their fire on the Salt Lake. On moving to the rear of Chocolate Hill, I saw a mass of men advancing in artillery formation across the lake. The Turkish batteries plastered the gallant Yeomen with shrapnel, causing some casualties, but they never lost their formation and kept steadily on until they obtained cover behind Chocolate Hill.

Here the 2nd Brigade under Lord Longford moved towards the left to a position in front of Scimitar Hill. Its advance was slow, hampered by the burning scrub and the confused jumble of men of the 29th and 11th Divisions, who had been driven off the summit.

The 1st Brigade under General Wiggin seems to have remained behind Chocolate Hill without orders, and to have taken but small part in the engagement. The 4th Brigade under General Taylor moved to the support of the 11th Division in the plain south-east of Chocolate Hill, and the 3rd Brigade under General McKenna, V.C., also moved to the south, but seems to have been held in reserve. It was nearly 7 p.m., and night was already setting in, when the 2nd Brigade reached the foot of Scimitar Hill.

Then came the final scene of this tragic day. It was almost impossible to see what was happening through the gathering gloom and smoke, only relieved by the bursting shells and flames. Just as darkness settled over the scene,

I distinguished a mass of men surging once again towards the summit of this dreadful hill. I have no idea who took part in this final advance. Probably the Dorsets and Yeomanry Brigade were joined by the remnants of the 29th and men of the 11th Divisions who were lying in the scrub at its foot. The mob surged upwards. The roar of the guns, the crackle of the rifle fire, the burr of the machine guns, was incessant, and then these blurred khaki figures disappeared in the darkness and smoke and were lost to view. Once again we thought that the hill had been won. But in reality it was impossible to hold the crest under the withering fire of shrapnel, rifle, and machine guns. The whole position was evacuated during the night. Not a yard of the enemy's trenches had been taken.

I left the battlefield at 8 p.m., stripped bare, with nothing left but my trousers and shirt. It came about in this way. About 5.30, the Turkish artillery fire on Chocolate Hill having diminished, I endeavoured to set up my cinema above the parapet of the partly destroyed trench to get some pictures of the wonderful panorama of the shellfire and burning scrub. The gunners were on me like a flash. I could not believe that they could have picked up a target so quickly. One shell whizzed past my head and stuck in the back of the trench without exploding. Then came another. I saw a bright flash and found myself in total darkness. I struggled to get clear but realised that I was buried. Shortly afterwards a spot of light appeared and I became conscious that I was being dug out. My benefactor turned out to be a soldier who had seen my mishap and who immediately ran to my assistance. I found the fuse of a high explosive shell lying on my legs but I had not received a scratch. My belongings did not fare so well. Owing to the heat, I had taken off my coat and placed it beside me with my small camera, walking-stick, field glasses, and water-bottle. They were probably blown to smithereens, and, in any case, disappeared for ever. The infernal old cinema, of which I was now heartily tired, the cause of all my troubles, had, of course, survived and I was reluctantly compelled to drag it back to camp.

Ellis Ashmead-Bartlett, *The Uncensored Dardanelles* (Hutchinson, 1928)

Chapter 3

GETTING STARTED

This chapter offers basic guidance for readers interested in researching either individual soldiers or the units in which they served in Gallipoli.

ONLINE RESOURCES

There are four major data providers with significant First World War content online: Ancestry, Findmypast, Military Genealogy and The National Archives. Ancestry (www.ancestry.co.uk) is undoubtedly the best place to start. It is a subscription site: you pay for a year's unlimited access to the data. If you are not already a subscriber, it is worth trying the free fourteen-day trial. Alternatively, access is free at many local libraries. However, Ancestry is of little use if your interest is not primarily genealogical. With the exception of the Medal Index Cards, much the same material is available on Findmypast (www.findmypast. co.uk), although it also has one or two unique resources of its own. At the time of writing (2014) the Military and Naval Archives website (www.NMarchives.com), from Naval & Military Press is about to launch, promising access to a number of First World War resources, including war diaries and medal rolls. The National Archives provides online access to service records for men who served in the Royal Navy and the Royal Air Force, and for the few women who joined the services during the war. There is also the Forces War Records. It is hard to know exactly what is available for the First World War, but it is unlikely it will have any of the key databases.

Not everything is online by any means. Particularly if you decide to do an in-depth study of an individual, or research a particular unit or action, you will probably need to use original papers, letters and files that are only to be found in an archive. If you want to know more about what archives are and how to use them, a series of Quick Animated Guides is available at www.nationalarchives.gov.uk/records/quick-animated-guides.htm.

There are three major types of archive with some overlap between their holdings. The most important is The National Archives (TNA) in Kew, which has almost all the surviving service and operational records for the three services plus much else besides. In this book any records mentioned are held by The National Archives (TNA) unless indicated otherwise. There is an excellent website – www.nationalarchives.gov.uk – which will help you find the records you are looking for and prepare for a visit. In particular, Research Signposts, and the more detailed Research Guides, explain the records very simply. Find them at www.nationalarchives.gov.uk/records.

The records themselves are described via the Discovery catalogue, which lists all eleven million documents available for researchers at Kew. The descriptions are often pretty general, but should be good enough for you to work out which are likely to be useful to you.

Regimental and service museums and archives have records relating to their particular regiment or service. The big service museums are the Imperial War Museum (for all services), the National Army Museum, the Royal Naval Museum (officially the National Museum of the Royal Navy (Portsmouth)), and the RAF Museum.

In addition, most regiments have their own regimental museum and archive, although their archives are increasingly likely to be found at the appropriate county record office. These archives may include collections of regimental orders, personal papers and photographs, war diaries (which may duplicate those at Kew), regimental magazines, registers and records which TNA for one reason or another did not want. All these archives have very different collections, so you may strike lucky or go away almost empty-handed. Most welcome visitors, but you usually have to make an appointment. The Army Museum Ogilby Trust maintains a very good website (www.armymuseums.org.uk) that links to museum websites and provides details about individual regimental museums.

Service and regimental museums do not have any service records: these are either at TNA or, for men who left after the end of 1920, with the Ministry of Defence.

County archives (or record offices) are also likely to have some material, particularly relating to the impact of the war on local communities. A few have the regimental archives deposited by the local regiment. There may also be records of local territorial regiments, which provided many of the troops who fought at Gallipoli.

There are also many more specialist repositories ranging from the British Library, which is comparable to The National Archives in size and importance, to company and hospital archives. With the exception of the British Library, which has records of the Indian Army, they are not likely to hold much direct information about the campaign in Gallipoli.

To find the addresses, websites and other contact details of all British (and some overseas) archives visit ARCHON – www.nationalarchives.gov.uk/archon – where there are links to individual archives websites. For regimental museums, however, it may be easier to go via www.armymuseums.org.uk.

There are two national databases showing which records are held where. The National Register of Archives (www.national archives.gov.uk/nra) offers broad descriptions of particular collections of records held at archives across the United Kingdom – this is particularly useful if you are looking to see whether there are papers for an individual or company. In addition, Access to

Archives (www.nationalarchives.gov.uk/a2a) offers more detailed descriptions of the holdings of many archives in England. This might be more useful in searching for generic references to Gallipoli or the Dardanelles, rather than for the records of an individual. There is also an equivalent for Wales (www.archives networkwales.info), while in Scotland the Scottish Archive Network provides something similar at www.scan.org.uk.

Using online catalogues can be tricky, particularly those provided by local record offices, so if there are any instructions it is a good idea to read them before you start. In general, the more information you type in, the more it will confuse the search engine, so try to keep it simple.

DEATH AND THE FLIES

In this extract from *The Secret Battle* (1919), Sir Alan Herbert describes life in a trench:

There was a great muddle in front. Troops of two different brigades were hopelessly entangled in the shallow trenches they had taken from the Turks. They had few officers left, and their staffs had the most imperfect impressions of the whereabouts of their mangled commands. So the sun was well up when we finally took over the line; this was in defiance of all tradition, but the Turk was shaken and did not molest us. The men who passed us on their way down grimly wished us joy of what they had left; their faces were pale and drawn, full of loathing and weariness, but they said little; and the impression grew that there was something up there which they could not even begin to describe. It was a still, scorching morning, and as we moved on the air became heavy with a sickening stench, the most awful of all smells that man can be called to endure, because it preyed on the imagination as well as the senses. For we knew now what it was.

We came into a Turkish trench, broad and shallow. In the first bay lay two bodies – a Lowlander and a Turk. They lay where they had killed each other, and they were very foul and loathsome in the sun. A man looked up at them and passed on, thinking, 'Glad I haven't got to stay here.' In the next bay there were three dead, all Englishmen; and in the next there were more and he thought, 'It was a hot fight just here.' But as he moved on, and in each succeeding bay beheld the same corrupt aftermath of yesterday's battle, the suspicion came to him that this was no local horror. Over the whole front of the attack, along two lines of trenches, these regiments of dead were everywhere found, strung in unnatural heaps along the parapets, or sprawling horribly half into the trench so that he touched them as he passed. Yet still he could not believe, and at each corner thought, 'Surely there will be none in this bay.'

But always there were more; until, if he were not careful or very callous, it began to get on his nerves, so that at the traverses he almost prayed that there might be no more beyond. Yet many did not realize what was before them till they were finally posted in the bays they were to garrison – three or four in a bay. Then they looked up at the sprawling horrors on the parapet and behind them — just above their heads, and knew that these were to be their close companions all that sweltering day, and perhaps beyond.

The regiment we had relieved had been too exhausted by the attack, or too short-handed, to bury more than a few, and the Turkish snipers made it impossible to do anything during the day. And so we sat all the scorching hours of the sun, or moved listlessly up and down, trying not to look upwards.

But there was a hideous fascination about the things, so that after a few hours a man came to know the bodies in his bay with a sickening intimacy, and could have told you many details about each of them – their regiment, and how they lay, and how they had died, and little things about their uniforms, a missing button, or some papers, or an old photograph sticking out of a pocket.

All of them were alive with flies, and at noon when we took out our bread and began to eat, the flies rose in a great black swarm and fell upon the food in our hands. After that no one could eat. All day men were being sent away by the doctor, stricken with sheer nausea by the flies and the stench and the things they saw, and went retching down the trench. To keep away the awful reek we went about for a little in the old gas-helmets, but the heat and burden of them in the hot, airless trench was intolerable.

The officers had no dug-outs, but sat under the parapets, like the men. No officer went sick; no officer could be spared; and indeed we seemed to have a greater power of resistance to this ordeal of disgust than the men ... all night we laboured at the burying of the bodies. It was bad work, every man who could be spared took his part, careless of sleep or rest, so long as he should but so strong was the horror upon us that we could not sit for another day with those things. But we could only bury half of them that night, and all the next day we went again through that lingering torment. And in the afternoon when we had orders to go up to the front line after dusk for an attack, we were glad. It was one of the very few moments in my experience when the war correspondent's legend of a regiment's pleasure at the prospect of battle came true. For anything was welcome if only we could get out of that trench, away from the smell and the flies, away from those bodies.

Chapter 4

RESEARCHING BRITISH SOLDIERS AND SAILORS

In this section we look at the basic records you can use to obtain a general picture of your ancestors' service.

Around half a million men served at some stage at Gallipoli or in the neighbouring waters, and although some records are missing you should be able to find something about each of them. However, exactly what is available cannot be predicted with any certainty, although there is more about the infantry and those who were killed or died of wounds than about men who served in supporting occupations.

All the men were volunteers. Some had been soldiers in the pre-war army, such as the men of the 1st Battalion, Lancashire Fusiliers, who led the landing on V Beach on 25 April and suffered terrible casualties in doing so. Others were members of the pre-war Territorial Force, or reservists who had been recalled to the colours on the outbreak of war. Many, however, had volunteered in the early weeks of the war and joined one of the new battalions that were urgently formed to cope with the flood of young men desirous of fighting the Kaiser.

Few of the Anzacs, for example, had any previous military experience, which makes their achievements all the more remarkable. Take the stretcher-bearer John Simpson, who achieved renown through carrying wounded Anzacs on a donkey in the early days of the landing; he had deserted from a British merchant navy ship and tramped around Australia looking for work before enlisting on 23 August 1914 in Perth. Like many British-born volunteers he had joined up so that he could get free passage to Britain in order to see his family.

GETTING STARTED

Before you start your research you need to be reasonably confident of the soldier's full name, the regiment or arm he served with, and his service number (if he was an ordinary soldier or non-commissioned officer). Otherwise it is very easy to start researching the wrong person.

If you have his medals, the information should be stamped on the rim or reverse. It may appear on any family papers, such as letters and diaries, or may even be written on the backs of photographs. Family stories can also help, although general statements such as 'he was at Gallipoli' or 'he was in the trenches when he was buried by an explosion' are obviously not very useful. Even so they may offer a clue.

MEDAL INDEX CARDS

Every serviceman and woman (as well as a few civilians) who saw service overseas was entitled to two campaign medals: the British War Medal and the Victory Medal. In addition, men who served overseas, including of course at Gallipoli, before 31 December 1915 were entitled to the 1914/15 Star. Each medal was embossed with the man's name and rank and number current at the time of his discharge.

There are several designs of Medal Index Card, but they should all tell you: the rank the man held at the end of his service, regimental numbers (other ranks only) and the units he served in, and the medals to which he was entitled, together with the place on the medal roll where details are to be found. In addition, the card should give the theatre of operations in which he first saw service. In most cases the card will be marked Gallipoli (or

Balkans), or possibly the code 2B. The date given should be the day that he landed on Gallipoli (that is, between 25 April 1915 and 8 January 1916), but if an earlier date is given then it may be when the man arrived in Egypt or came via the Western Front.

There may be additional information such as his date of discharge (or the date of his death in action), any gallantry medals he was awarded, perhaps a note that he was entitled to wear the oak leaf emblem on the Victory Medal for being Mentioned in Despatches, usually abbreviated to EMB (for emblem), and whether he was discharged to the Z Reserve in 1919 – that is, he could be recalled in the event of the resumption of hostilities.

The Cards are available online at both Ancestry ('British Army WWI Medal Rolls Index Cards') and via The National Archives website. Of the two, Ancestry offers by far the better reproduction in colour and provides both sides of each card, which occasionally includes the address to which the medals were sent. In addition, summaries providing details of the units with which a man served and his regimental numbers are available through Findmypast and the Lives of the First World War project free of charge, although they aren't all that easy to find. Details are available at: www.livesofthefirst worldwar.org.

The medal rolls themselves are at The National Archives in series WO 329 and online at www.NMarchives.com. They are probably not worth consulting as the only additional information you are likely to find is the infantry battalion in which he was serving at the time of his death or discharge. However, this may help you find the appropriate battalion war diary.

SILVER WAR BADGE

You may also come across a card for the Silver War Badge. A small, circular lapel badge made of sterling silver, it bore the king's initials, a crown, and the inscriptions 'For King and Empire' and 'Services Rendered'. The Silver War Badge provided former soldiers with some form of identification to show that they had faithfully served King and Country before their honorable discharge. Medal rolls are also available on Ancestry, but they are not very informative.

SERVICE RECORDS: OTHER RANKS AND NON-COMMISSIONED OFFICERS

Service records can be a key resource in tracing an individual serviceman, supplying details of postings, wounds and sickness, and perhaps some family details. Unfortunately, however, less than a third of service records survive. The remainder were destroyed during the Blitz.

Individual files contain a wide variety of documents, which can be informative if at times a little bewildering; with a little practice and patience you should be able to decipher the forms and build up an intimate portrait of the individual. They certainly repay close study.

No two files are the same. Some are very detailed, with a variety of forms, letters and other paperwork, but in other cases you may find only a man's attestation form or perhaps a medical record. Of particular importance is the attestation form that was completed by the individual on enlistment. This indicates when and where a man enlisted and was discharged, and gives other personal details such as civilian occupation, home address and date of birth. It usually appears at the beginning of a service record. Files for pre-war regular soldiers, part-time members of the Territorial Army, or reservists recalled to the colours include their pre-war attestation forms and details of their pre-war service, which might occasionally go back to the Boer War or earlier.

The other document to look out for is Form B103/1 'Casualty Form – Active Service'. Despite the name, it includes far more than information on wounds and hospital stays. It could also tell you about promotions through the ranks (and demotions if appropriate), and list the units he served in; it may indicate when he went overseas and when he returned to Britain to be discharged; it may provide details of any medical treatments received and perhaps notes of any disciplinary offences (generally for drunkenness, petty theft or ignoring an officer's order). You may also find the date and reason for death.

If a man died during his army service, there may well be correspondence and forms about his will and personal effects, as well as perhaps letters from his next of kin seeking more information about the circumstances of his loss.

What these records do not do is to tell you very much about any fighting he was engaged in or any gallantry medals he may have received, nor can they offer any real idea about his life in the army. However, you can use the war diaries to obtain this information.

These service records are online at both Ancestry and Findmypast. The service records of men who continued to serve in the army after the end of 1920 are still with the Ministry of Defence. Full details are available at www.veterans-uk.info.

OFFICERS' SERVICE RECORDS

Surviving service records are at The National Archives in series WO 339 and WO 374. About 85 per cent have survived. In practice, there seems to be little difference between the two series. There is just one file for each officer, and they are not online.

At some stage the records were weeded and much material was destroyed. Records for men who survived are generally less full than those for men who died in action. Even so, there may be correspondence concerning money, length of service and pensions, rather than directly about an individual's war service. If an officer came through the ranks, then there should be his original enlistment document and recommendations from his commanding officer. If a man died during his service there are likely to be papers relating to the administration of his will and dispersal of his effects, as well as correspondence with the next of kin, who were often desperate to discover the circumstances of their son, brother or husband's death. The files of both Captain Clem Attlee and Lieutenant John Still contain medical board reports as both men had been injured during the course of their service.

Officers are listed in the Army Lists. These provide an easy way to confirm whether an ancestor was an officer or not, because the Lists include everyone who was commissioned, giving details about which regiment or unit he was with, his rank and when he was promoted to it. They are available online at the Internet Archive at www.archive.org, although they are not particularly easy to use. The commercial genealogical data providers may offer the occasional copy. In addition, complete sets can be found in the Open Reading Room at The National Archives and at the IWM, the British Library and the National Army Museum.

The *London Gazette* is the government's official newspaper. It includes announcements of the appointment of officers and any subsequent promotions, together with when and how they were discharged. The surnames and initials of individual officers are given, together with their regiment and the date of the promotion (even temporary ones). Inevitably, publication may have taken place months after the event, but the date the promotion was granted is always given. A brief reason for a resignation is often given. The *London Gazette* has been digitised and is online at www.thegazette.co.uk. The indexing, however, is rather erratic.

Identifying Military Uniforms

You may have photographs showing the soldier/s you are researching in uniform. As well as providing a direct link to the past, such photographs can tell you something about his service through the insignia and badges shown.

Officers and other ranks wore differently designed uniforms, and it is always clear which was which. Officers' uniforms were better tailored, and officers were rarely seen without a tie. Ordinary soldiers wore coarser tunics and trousers (kilts, of course, in the Highland regiments). Non-commissioned officers wore downward pointing chevrons (one for a lance corporal, two for a corporal and three for a sergeant) on each arm above the elbow. (They should not be confused with long-service stripes, which are found below the elbow.)

Each regiment and corps had its own badge worn on the cap or as buttons on the jacket and tunic. A few are very distinctive, such as the mounted gun for the Royal Artillery or the flaming grenade of the Grenadier Guards, but most at first glance look very similar.

There are various guides to help you decipher your photographs. The best books are Neil Storey, *Military Photographs and How to Date Them* (Countryside Books, 2010) and Robert Pols, *Identifying Old Army Photographs* (Family History Partnership, 2011). For regimental badges, see Ian Swinnerton's *Identifying Your World War I Soldier from Badges and Photographs* (Family History Partnership, 2004) and Peter Doyle and Chris Foster's *British Army Cap Badges of the First World War* (Shire, 2010). Probably the best general introduction to interpreting uniforms is provided by Chris McDonald at www.4thgordons.com/I-Spybook%20of%20Uniforms1.2.pdf. There are several rather unsatisfactory websites that may help you to identify regimental badges; the best is probably the British Armed Services and National Service site at www.britisharmedforces.org/index.php

CASUALTIES

Just over 700,000 British men and a few dozen women were killed during the First World War and many hundreds of thousands more received some form of medical treatment. During the

Wounded men lying in Gully Ravine. The ravine was the centre of a major action at the end of June 1915.

Gallipoli campaign nearly 60,000 Allied troops lost their lives and over 120,000 were wounded in some way.

This can be broken down as follows:

Country	Deaths	Wounded	Taken Prisoner	Total
United Kingdom	34,072	78,520	7,654	120,246
France	9,798	17,371		27,169
Australia	8,709	19,441		28,150
New Zealand	2,721	4,752		7,473
Newfoundland	49	93		142
India	1,358	3,421		4,779
TOTAL	**56,707**	**123,598**	**7,654**	**187,959**

On the Ottoman side, there were 56,643 deaths and 107,007 men wounded. In addition 11,178 men were made prisoners of war.

Each of the 46,909 British and Commonwealth deaths is commemorated by the Commonwealth War Graves Commission. The Commission maintains cemeteries in 150 countries across the world. You can find more about its work and its history on its website: www.cwgc.org.

There are thirty-one cemeteries on the Gallipoli peninsula: six at Helles (plus the only solitary grave: that of Lieutenant Colonel Charles Doughty-Wylie VC, Royal Welch Fusiliers), four at Suvla and twenty-one at Anzac. Many of those killed in action, and those who died on hospital ships and were buried at sea, have no known grave. These men's names are recorded on one of five memorials to the missing: the Lone Pine Memorial commemorates Australians killed in the Anzac sector, as well as New Zealanders with no known grave or who were buried at sea, while the Lone Pine, Hill 60 and Chunuk Bair Memorials commemorate New Zealanders who died at Anzac. There is also a memorial at Twelve Tree Copse Cemetery commemorating the New Zealanders killed in the Helles sector, while British, Indian and Australian troops who died there are commemorated on the Helles Memorial at the tip of Cape Helles. This is the largest memorial, with 21,000 names inscribed on panels around a 30-metre-high obelisk. There are two more CWGC cemeteries on the Greek island of Limnos. This was the hospital base for the Allied forces in Gallipoli and most of the men buried here were those who had died of their wounds.

A database of war deaths is also available through the CWGC website. It is one of the key resources for First World War research and is very easy to use. You can search by name, regiment or cemetery, and filter searches by service, nationality or year of death.

For each individual the register will tell you: the name that appears on the gravestone (generally, but not always, a man's full

The Aquitania *was a pre-war Atlantic liner, which was converted into a hospital ship during the Dardanelles Campaign. She carried several thousand sick and wounded men to hospitals in Malta or even back to England.*

name); the date of his death; his age (if known) and nationality; his rank, service number (if appropriate) and the unit to which he belonged; and the cemetery and plot number where he is buried or, for men who have no known grave, the plaque on the appropriate memorial to the missing on which his name has been engraved.

In addition, there may also be a brief note about a man's parents or wife, any special inscription chosen by the family for his grave, and perhaps whether he was attached to another regiment at the time of death. For Captain Owen Day of the 2nd Hampshires, who was killed on 6 August, there is a note that he was the 'son of Arthur James Day and Georgiana, his wife, of 17, Archers Rd., Southampton'. This additional information was supplied by the family as the Commission contacted relatives to give them the opportunity to add personal details. The Commission is currently digitising its archives, and some additional information should be online by the time this book is published.

The exact location of a grave in any Commonwealth War Graves Commission cemetery is indicated after the entry by a series of letters and numbers. The initial Roman numeral indicates the plot, while the row within that plot is specified by a capital letter and the individual grave by a number. Thus II B 28 indicates plot II, row B, grave 28. In the registers of cemeteries that are not divided into plots, the row is indicated by a capital letter following the entry and the grave by a number. Thus D 12 indicates Row D, Grave 12.

It is possible to obtain photographs of war graves without visiting the cemeteries by contacting The War Graves Photographic Project (http://twgpp.org). The website includes an index which allows you to see whether there is already a photograph of the grave you are interested in. If there is, you can call up a low resolution image of the gravestone (or entry on the appropriate memorial for men who have no known grave). You can also obtain a high resolution image of the stone for a donation. They recommend a very reasonable £3.50. More details are, of course, on the website.

SOLDIERS DIED IN THE GREAT WAR

A little more information can be found in the Soldiers Died in the Great War databases available through both Ancestry and Findmypast. This list was originally compiled after the Armistice by the War Office. Soldiers Died contains additional details to those provided by the Commonwealth War Graves Commission, notably the place and date of enlistment and home address.

Sometimes a birth place is given, as well as a brief description of how they died, usually 'killed in action', but sometimes 'died of wounds'.

ROLLS OF HONOUR

One phenomenon that arose out of the war was the roll of honour: a published list of the deceased (and occasionally other groups of servicemen such as prisoners of war). Rolls are often available for workplaces (including local councils and railway companies), chapels and small communities. They are definitely worth looking out for, although in most cases the information they contain can as easily be obtained from the Commonwealth War Graves Commission or Soldiers Died in the Great War databases.

There is no nationwide set of these rolls, although the Imperial War Museum and British Library almost certainly have the largest collections. Archives and local study libraries may have copies of rolls for their area. A number have been republished by the Naval & Military Press (www.naval-military-press.com).

There are several national rolls. Entries for some 26,000 officers and other ranks (including 7,000 photographs) were collected and published in 1917 by the Marquis Melville de Ruvigny, a noted genealogist of the period. *De Ruvigny's Roll of Honour: A Biographical Record of His Majesty's Military and Aerial Forces Who Fell in the Great War 1914–1917* is available on Ancestry and Findmypast, but is often overlooked by researchers. There is, for example, a detailed biography of Captain Owen Day of the 2nd Hampshires, including a photograph and a description of how he gallantly met his death attacking enemy trenches.

After the war some tens of thousands of war memorials were erected in honour of the men who did not return. They are still common features in towns and villages. As well as those commemorating the dead from a particular town or area, there are many memorials for schools, churches or work places.

The UK National Inventory of War Memorials at the Imperial War Museum has prepared a database of some 55,000 memorials at www.ukniwm.org.uk, of which 488 are dedicated to the men and units that fought at Gallipoli, ranging from a general plaque in St Paul's Cathedral to a stained-glass triptych dedicated to Captain Owen Heathcote Lacy Day of the 2nd Hampshire Regiment, which was originally in St Mary's Church, Southampton. Day was killed on 6 August 1915 and he lies buried at Twelve Trees Copse Cemetery. The results may include a full transcript of the dedication, a physical description of the memorial, and an account of why and how it came to be created. Sometimes there is a photograph as well. An increasing number of entries include listings of all the individuals commemorated on the memorial.

If you are researching an Irish soldier or unit, check out the Irish War Memorials website (www.irishwarmemorials.ie), which lists many memorials to the fallen in both the North and the South, and there are indexes both to individuals and to places.

Scotland's war dead are honoured at the Scots National War Memorial at Edinburgh Castle. More information can be found at www.snwm.org.

HOSPITAL RECORDS

If the service record for your man survives, it should contain a Casualty Form (Form B103) which will record visits to the doctor, admissions to hospital and so on. Of course, many entries mention war-related wounds, but a surprising number of entries concern everyday ailments and complaints. The forms can sometimes be difficult to decode because they also contain details of postings, promotions and demotions, as well as punishments.

An efficient system for dealing with casualties was quickly introduced on the outbreak of war to ferry the sick and wounded to the appropriate casualty clearing station or hospital in the rear.

Certainly this was the case on the Western Front, where the system considerably reduced the number of deaths.

On Gallipoli the position was somewhat different. Here the medical resources were inadequate, and the situation was not helped by the fact that the terrain and the close nature of the fighting made it difficult to carry the wounded back to the casualty clearing stations, let alone to the beaches from where they were ferried to the waiting hospital ships. One of the most iconic images of the campaign for Australians is 'Simpson and his donkey'. John Simpson was a stretcher-bearer in the Australian Army Medical Corps. Using one of the donkeys brought in for carrying water, he transported wounded men day and night from the fighting in Monash Valley to the beach on Anzac Cove. He did so, according to the Australian official historian Charles Bean, despite 'deadly sniping down the valley and the most furious shrapnel fire'. He was killed by machine-gun fire while carrying two wounded men on 19 May and was buried on the beach at Hell Spit. The war diary of the 3rd Field Ambulance commended 'the excellence of the work performed by Pte Simpson continuously since landing'. Simpson was posthumously Mentioned in Despatches.

A card was completed for each man, which accompanied him at all times, but the records (with the exception of a small sample) have long since been destroyed. The National Archives has samples of a few medical-related and hospital admission records in series MH 106. Among them can be found nine admissions and discharge books for the hospital ship Assaye, which evacuated casualties from Cape Helles, Anzac and Suvla Bay. The books contain details of men's names, unit and rank, as well as the injuries they had suffered. A few medical operations were also carried out on board, and these are briefly listed by type and outcome. If a death occurred this is also recorded, and in rare instances the latitude and longitude are given if the man was buried at sea. At the time of writing the registers are being

An iconic shot of an Anzac soldier carrying a wounded comrade to a dressing station.

digitised and, with luck, they should be available on the Forces Records website by the time this book has been published.

Sue Light has an excellent guide to medical records at www.scarletfinders.co.uk/125.htm.

A dressing station at Suvla Beach. Here men were either treated or made ready for transfer to a hospital ship.

GALLANTRY MEDALS

Gallantry medals were awarded for acts of heroism and bravery on the field of battle. Some medals were awarded immediately for special acts (sometimes referred to as being awarded 'in the field'), while others – known as non-immediate – might be awarded weeks or months after the act. Inevitably medals were issued on an almost indiscriminate basis: some men who won them probably did not deserve them, while other men's heroic acts remained unrecognised. Tim Travers cites the example of Private Albert Wilkin of the 7th Royal Dublin Fusiliers, who was bravely defending his position against a rain of Turkish bombs. He courageously threw several bombs back before they could explode, but the fifth one he picked up exploded, blowing him to pieces.

The best known gallantry medal is undoubtedly the Victoria Cross. A register of VC winners can be found in series WO 98 at Kew, together with copies of their citations, and other information is also available online on Discovery. Details of the three dozen VC winners at Gallipoli is given at www.gallipoli-association.org/content/men-of-gallipoli/gallipoli-vc's. More information about each of the winners and how they won the award is given in Gerald Gliddon, *VCs of the First World War: the Side Shows* (The History Press, 2014).

The Distinguished Service Order (DSO) was normally awarded only to senior officers, while the Military Cross (MC) was awarded for acts of bravery to officers of the rank of captain or below. The equivalents for non-commissioned officers and other ranks were the Distinguished Conduct Medal (DCM) and Military Medal (MM).

In many cases non-immediate gallantry awards were given out almost randomly to members of a platoon or company who had seen action. Often men were asked to nominate comrades who should be honoured.

If there isn't a family story about the award of a gallantry medal, or you have the medal itself, there may be a note on the Medal Index Card or, more rarely, in the service record. Details of all gallantry awards were published in the London Gazette, sometimes with a citation (that is, a short description of why the medal was awarded). At the very least you will find the man's name, service number (not officers), rank, regiment and the date when the award was made. For awards of the Military Medal (MM), this is the only information you are likely to find. If your man was in the Royal Artillery, Findmypast has a list of RA men who won the Military Medal with the date their award was gazetted. Citations for awards of the Distinguished Conduct Medal (DCM) can be found on both Ancestry and Findmypast.

They usually duplicate what is in the *London Gazette* but are certainly easier to use.

If you are lucky, you may be able to work out exactly why the medal was awarded from the war diaries. In addition, the awarding of gallantry medals to both officers and other ranks is often mentioned in war diaries.

There are also some Medal Index Cards for men awarded the DCM and MM. They give little more than the date and page number in the *London Gazette* where the award is listed, but beware: in my experience the reference is often wrong.

The award of gallantry medals awards may well feature in newspaper stories. The most common award was the Mention in Despatches (MiD) for acts of bravery or service that warranted reward, but was not enough to merit a gallantry award. Awards are listed in the London Gazette. The fact that a man was awarded a MiD is usually shown on the Medal Index Card (often abbreviated to EM or EMB with a date when the award was published in the *Gazette*). There may also be separate cards with the approximate date the award was gazetted.

Further Reading
More about medals (both gallantry and campaign) can be found in Peter Duckers, *British Military Medals: a Guide for Collectors and Researchers* (2nd edn, Pen & Sword, 2013). Also useful is the *Medals Yearbook* published annually by Token Publishing.

Courts Martial

Nearly 300,000 soldiers and 6,000 officers faced courts martial during the war, generally for being absent without leave, petty theft or drunkenness. The Casualty Form in the service record reports any misdemeanours and should indicate whether your ancestor was put on a charge. Registers of courts martial in WO 90 (for men serving overseas) and WO 92 (for men on home duty) give brief details of the offence. Crime in Gallipoli was very low because there was little opportunity for thieving or getting drunk. The most serious problem was soldiers harming themselves in an attempt to get sent to Egypt or back to Britain to recover.

PRISONERS OF WAR

Nearly eight thousand British men were captured by the Turks during the campaign. Conditions were undoubtedly grim in the prisoner of war camps. Many prisoners came to depend largely on Red Cross parcels, which were collected and packed by voluntary organisations under the leadership of the British Red Cross.

The International Committee of the Red Cross (ICRC) in Geneva was responsible for passing details of prisoners of war between the various combatant nations and ensuring that conditions in the camps were adequate. The Committee collected, analysed and classified information it received from the detaining powers and national agencies about prisoners of war and civilian internees. It compared this information with requests submitted to it by relatives or friends, in order to restore contact between them. The ICRC's collections consist of some 500,000 pages of lists and six million index cards. These are now online at www.icrc.org.

However, it is difficult to find out very much about individual POWs in British archives, as the records have largely been destroyed. A list of prisoners in German and Turkish hands in 1916 can be found in AIR 1/892/204/5/696-698 at Kew, which indicates where a prisoner was captured and when, where they were held and their next of kin. There is a published *List of Officers taken Prisoner in the Various Theatres of War* between August 1914 and November 1918 (1919, reprinted 1988), which is with Findmypast.

If you are researching an officer, there may be a report about the circumstances of his capture by the enemy, submitted by the man to an official board of enquiry. That for Lieutenant John Still of the 6th East Yorkshire Regiment, who was taken prisoner during the shambolic attack on Takke Tape hill northeast of Anzac, reads:

> The [Bn] attacked the hill Takke Tape at dawn on 9 August 1915. There was heavy fire from front and flank. I accompanied Lt Col Moore, CO of the battalion with the leading company. About thirty of us reached the top of the hill, unsupported, and found it strongly held. We retreated down a deep, narrow, winding ravine, with the intention of joining up with the remainder of the battalion which we expected to find at the bottom of the hill, some 900 feet below and a mile away. Only five reached the foot of the hill alive, viz Lt Col Moore, Capt R D Elliott, Cpl Blanchflower, Pte Moor and myself. There we were attacked by a considerable body of Turks in between us and the plain. The Colonel told me to make signals of surrender. While doing this I was hit. The Colonel was bayonetted very shortly afterwards and the other four were taken prisoner. [WO 339/23842]

Still later wrote a book about his experiences as a prisoner of war: *Prisoner of the Turks* (1920), which remains one of the few accounts of the treatment of POWs in the Middle East.

Further Reading
Sarah Paterson, *Tracing Your First World War Prisoners of War* (Pen & Sword, 2012).

PENSIONS
Widows and disabled ex-servicemen were entitled to claim a pension. Much ill-feeling was created by the low level of the pension and the difficulties placed in the way of claimants by the government and local officials supervising the grant of awards.

Most records have long since been destroyed. However, series PIN 82 at Kew contains an 8 per cent sample of widows' and dependents' papers arranged in alphabetical order. The forms give personal details of each serviceman's name, place of residence, particulars of service and the date, place and cause of death or injury. They also give details of the assessment of, and entitlement to, pension awards, the amount awarded, and the length of time for which the award was granted.

There is a set of post-war pension appeal records at the National Records of Scotland (www.nrscotland.gov.uk) in series PT6. The records contain detailed pension applications from thousands of Scottish soldiers and their next of kin (usually widows).

The Western Front Association (WFA) recently rescued a series of pension cards relating to the granting of pensions and other payments to soldiers and their dependents. As with all records from the First World War, the content varies greatly between individuals but you may expect to find material about the individual and his family as well as the reason why payments were made. At present the records are being indexed by the Association, but they will do look-ups for enquirers for a small fee. You can find out more at www.westernfrontassociation. com/great-war-current-news/pension-records.html.

PERSONAL PAPERS AND EFFECTS

Soldiers (and indeed for that matter sailors and airmen) wrote about their experiences at the time in letters and diaries, and perhaps in old age they wrote up their memoirs. An increasing number are appearing in print or on websites. That they did this is not surprising: they were witnessing events unique in human history.

There was a very efficient postal service during the war. Most soldiers took advantage of this to write regular letters home. Because of official censorship and the soldiers' own desire not to frighten their families, such letters tend to be fairly anodyne, reassuring the reader that they were well, perhaps indicating that they were safe behind the lines, and often asking for items to be sent out. In general they are not great works of literature, but even so after nearly a century they are treasured family heirlooms.

Neither officers nor men were allowed to keep diaries, although clearly many did. Some were just simple entries about the weather and unit locations in a pocket diary, while others were much more elaborate affairs, such as the one kept by New Zealander Gunner Ralph Doughty. On 6 June, for example, he wrote:

9 am. Another good old go yesterday. Mechinson, Shepherd, Moore, Archer and Lee casualties. Their heavy guns played havoc amongst our troops. Firing on and off all night. Rec. a paper from C.A. Some of our boys rec. boxes of sweets etc. while Rowlings (Motueka) rec. a xmas cake while someone else had a bottle of wine. GREAT FEAST. Very rowdy morning. Got action before breakfast and kept a warm fire for an hour. Immediately afterwards got to it hot and strong. Our gun was detailed to keep reinforcements from getting to the firing line, via a small nullah [ravine]. And it did. We just waited for them to come over the far crest and they got it. We had them on toast alright. Couldn't advance or retreat and our guns cut off flanking movements by spraying each side with shrapnel. The only thing for them to do was to take cover in a bit of light scrub which they did and we got on to that scrub and searched every inch of it for 2 solid hours. I've just been to the observation station and had a look at it with the glasses. Not a man came out of it alive. The ground is packed thickly with them. Our Colonel, Major and a few more odds and ends performed the tango with great gusto. I am as deaf as a mule in the right ear and both hands burnt a bit. We're

having another go in a few minutes. Our Asiatic friends are paying particular 'H' just now, with their big mobile siege guns, one shell has landed 100 away, can't see anything for smoke. Shook the ground like an earthquake. Gnr Sanderson badly wounded. Fighting all night. [Ralph Doughty diaries, www.thekivellfamily.co.nz/military_history/ralphs_diaries/transcribes/diary_one_p5.html. Also quoted in Peter Hart, Gallipoli.]

Memoirs are also important. Some are based on diaries and letters or correspondence with old comrades, while others were clearly written decades later for the grandchildren or to lay old ghosts to rest. There are many accounts of the Gallipoli campaign which have been mined by writers like Peter Hart and Lyn Macdonald to bring their books alive.

In some cases there will be no memoirs at all, except perhaps some vague family stories, while others may have collections of medals, army service discharge papers, pay books and photographs. If you have such a collection it is well worth considering donating it to the Imperial War Museum or a local record office or regimental archive. They may be willing to give you a set of copies in return for the originals. Certainly you should think about making some provision for their care in your will.

There is no central list of what personal papers are to be found where, although it is worth checking the National Register of Archives to see whether a collection of papers has been identified (www.nationalarchives.gov.uk/nra).

The Imperial War Museum has the most important collections of personal papers. They are described in the Museum's catalogue at www.iwm.org.uk/collections/search.

Another important resource is the Liddle Collection at Leeds University's Brotherton Library, with over 4,000 collections of private papers: http://library.leeds.ac.uk/liddle-collection.

The Liddell Hart Archives at King's College (www.kcl.ac.uk/library/collections/archivespec/index.aspx) has papers for many former senior soldiers and sailors, including those of Sir Ian Hamilton. There is a list of their holdings for the First World War at www.kcl.ac.uk/library/collections/archivespec/catalogues/World WarOneguide01.aspx. Apart from a collection of photographs found in Sir Ian's papers there is little online.

Regimental archives and the National Army Museum are also good sources. The Royal Artillery Archives in Woolwich, for example, contains much for the First World War, particularly for officers. In addition, small collections can sometimes be found at local record offices.

Lastly, an increasing number of diaries and memoirs in particular are being published or are appearing online, such as Ralph Doughty's diary quoted above. Pen & Sword has published well over a hundred such memoirs, which you can buy direct at www.pen-and-sword.co.uk. Many others are available from the Naval & Military Press (www.naval-military-press.com).

The Imperial War Museum and other museums have impressive collections of ephemera, which in the case of the IWM itself can be seen in its online catalogue. Much of it is displayed in the new galleries at the Museum's London site.

A fascinating Europe-wide initiative to collect personal items from each of the participating nations, including letters, diaries, photographs and ephemera, is being collated by Europeana at www.europeana1914-1918.eu/en. It is a collection that deserves to be better known. Several hundred items relate to Gallipoli. The vast majority are from the UK and Ireland, but there is also material from France, Germany and Turkey. In addition, it is possible to search similar projects in Australia and New Zealand.

OTHER USEFUL GENEALOGICAL RECORDS
It is easy to overlook the basic genealogical sources of birth,

marriage and death records, census returns and wills in researching soldiers, but they are also worth checking out. And, of course, many researchers first become aware of having military ancestors from an entry in the census or on a marriage certificate. Most of these records are now available online.

THE CENSUS

Census records are an important source for family history, often revealing unique information about ancestors. In particular, because it was taken so close to the outbreak of the war, the 1911 census is a key source. The English and Welsh census is available through Findmypast and Ancestry. The Scottish 1911 census is at Scotlands People (www.scotlandspeople.gov.uk) and the Irish census is at www.census.nationalarchives.ie. The information in all three censuses is almost identical and they are fully indexed so it is easy to find an ancestor in it.

The 1911 census is unique for another reason. For the first time servicemen (and their families) serving overseas in both the navy and army were recorded, giving their name, age, rank and place of birth. Of particular interest are the returns for army wives and children. This is the first census for which such records exist. To access the military returns in the appropriate box on the search screen tick 'Overseas military'.

There are no Australian or New Zealand equivalents.

BIRTH, MARRIAGE AND DEATH CERTIFICATES

National registration began in England and Wales on 1 July 1837 (Scotland 1855, Ireland 1864) and the system has remained largely unchanged since then. You can order certificates for men who were killed in action or died of wounds during the war, but there is little point, as they won't tell you anything you don't know already.

English and Welsh certificates can be ordered online at www.gro.gov.uk/gro/content/certificates/default.asp or by phone on 0300 123 1837. Scottish records are all online through Scotland's People. Indexes to Irish births, marriages and deaths for the period (both North and South) are available through FamilySearch (www.familysearch.org), but you have to order the certificates from the General Register Office for Ireland (www.groireland.ie).

Also of interest are Chaplains' Returns and Army Register Books recording births, baptisms, marriages, deaths and burials of soldiers and their families at home and abroad. Indexes are at www.findmypast.com and at The National Archives in Kew.

WILLS

It was natural for soldiers to make their wills before going into action. Indeed, the army pay book, which was issued to all soldiers, included a simple will form that could be completed. Generally any possessions were left to the individual's wife or next of kin.

There may well be papers about wills and the disposal of personal effects in the files of individual officers and soldiers.

Details of wills proved in the Principal Probate Registry were published in the National Probate Calendars. The Calendars are online at Ancestry. Wills themselves cost £10 (at time of writing) and can be ordered by post from the Leeds District Probate Registry, York House, 31 York Place, Leeds LS1 2BA.

In addition, the Probate Registry has released details of some 200,000 wills that were made by soldiers in the field. There is an index at www.gov.uk/probate-search. You can order copies online for £10 each.

The National Records of Scotland has a collection of 26,000 wills for Scottish soldiers, which are available through the Scotlands People website. The Irish National Archives has some 9,000 wills available at http://soldierswills.nationalarchives.ie/search/sw/home.jsp.

LANDING ON GALLIPOLI

In this extract from his first novel *The Secret Battle (1919)*, Sir Alan Herbert describes the landing of a battalion on Gallipoli a few weeks after the landings on 25 April. Sir Alan served in the Royal Naval Division.

The sun went down, and soon it was very cold in the sweeper: and in each man's heart I think there was a certain chill. There were no more songs, but the men whispered in small groups, or stood silent, shifting uneasily their wearisome packs. For now we were indeed cut off from civilization and committed to the unknown. The transport we had left seemed a very haven of comfort and security; one thought longingly of white tables in the saloon, and the unfriendly linen bags of bully beef and biscuits we carried were concrete evidence of a new life. The war seemed no longer remote, and each of us realized indignantly that we were personally involved in it. So for a little all these soldiers had a period of serious thought unusual in the soldier's life.

But as we neared the Peninsula the excitement and novelty and the prospect of exercising cramped limbs brought back valour and cheerfulness. At Malta we had heard many tales of the still terrifying ordeal of landing under fire.

But such terrors were not for us. There was a bright moon, and as we saw the pale cliffs of Cape Helles, all, I think, expected each moment a torrent of shells from some obscure quarter. But instead an unearthly stillness brooded over the two bays, and only a Morse lamp blinking at the sweeper suggested that any living thing was there. And there came over the water a strange musty smell; some said it was the smell of the dead, and some the smell of an

The SS River Clyde *took hundreds of troops to W Beach in the early hours of 25 April. Subsequently beached, she became a temporary quay and breakwater as well as housing a dressing station in her hold.* ' V'Beach

incinerator; myself I do not know, but it was the smell of the Peninsula, which no man can forget.

We disembarked at a pier of rafts by the River Clyde, and stumbled eagerly ashore. And now we were in the very heart of heroic things. Nowhere, I think, was the new soldier plunged so suddenly into the genuine scenes of war as he was at Gallipoli; in France there was a long transition of training-camps and railway trains and billets, and he moved by easy gradations to the firing-line. But here, a few hours after a night in linen sheets, we stood suddenly on the very sand where, but three weeks before, those hideous machine-guns in the cliffs had mown down that astonishing party of April 25. And in that silver stillness it was difficult to believe. We stumbled off up the steady slope between two cliffs, marvelling that any men could have prevailed against so perfect a field of fire.

By now we were very tired, and it was heavy work labouring through the soft sand. Queer, Moorish-looking figures in white robes peered at us from dark corners, and here and there a man poked a tousled head from a hole in the ground, and blinked upon our progress. Someone remarked that it reminded him of nothing so much as the native camp at Earl's Court on a fine August evening, and that indeed was the effect. After a little the stillness was broken by a sound which we could not conceal from ourselves was the distant rattle of musketry; somewhere a gun fired startlingly; and now as we went each man felt vaguely that at any minute we might be plunged into the thick of battle, laden as we were, and I think each man braced himself for a desperate struggle. Such is the effect of marching in the dark to an unknown destination.

Soon we were halted in a piece of apparently waste land circled by trees, and ordered to dig ourselves a habitation at once, for 'in the morning' it was whispered 'the Turks search all this ground'. Everything was said in a kind of hoarse, mysterious whisper, presumably to conceal our observations from the ears of the Turks five miles away. But then we did not know they were five miles away; we had no idea where they were or where we were ourselves. Men glanced furtively at the North Star for guidance, and were pained to find that, contrary to their military teaching, it told them nothing. Even the digging was carried on a little stealthily till it was discovered that the Turks were not behind those trees.

The digging was a comfort to the men, who being

pitmen, were now in their element; and the officers found solace in whispering to each other that magical communication about the prospective 'searching'; it was the first technical word they had used in the field, and they were secretly proud to know what it meant.

In a little the dawn began, and the grey trees took shape; and the sun came up out of Asia, and we saw at last the little sugar-loaf peak of Achi Baba, absurdly pink and diminutive in the distance. A man's first frontal impression of that great rampart, with the outlying slopes masking the summit, was that it was disappointingly small; but when he had lived under and upon it for a while, day by day, it seemed to grow in menace and in bulk, and ultimately became a hideous, overpowering monster, pervading all his life; so that it worked upon men's nerves, while, day by day, it seemed to grow and almost everywhere in the Peninsula they were painfully conscious that every movement they made could be watched from somewhere on that massive hill. But now the kitchens had come, and there was breakfast and viscous, milkless tea.

We discovered that all around our seeming solitude the earth had been peopled with sleepers, who now emerged from their holes; there was a stir of washing and cooking and singing, and the smoke went up from the wood fires in the clear, cool air. D Company officers made their camp under an olive-tree, with a view over the blue water to Samothrace and Imbros , and now in the early cool, before the sun had gathered his noonday malignity, it was very pleasant. At seven o'clock the 'searching' began. A mile away, on the northern cliffs, the first shell burst, stampeding a number of horses. The long-drawn warning scream and the final crash gave all the expectant battalion a faintly pleasurable thrill, and as each shell came a little nearer the sensation remained. No one was afraid; without the knowledge of experience no one could be seriously afraid on this cool, sunny morning in the grove of olive trees.

Those chill hours in the sweeper had been much more alarming. The common sensation was: 'At last I am really under fire; to-day I shall write home and tell them about it.' And then, when it seemed that the line on which the shells were falling must, if continued, pass through the middle of our camp, the firing mysteriously ceased.

Chapter 5

RESEARCHING UNITS

STRUCTURE

During the First World War the British Army expanded from a fairly small organisation in July 1914 to a huge institution by the end of 1918, which historians have suggested was the biggest temporary organisation ever created in Britain. During the war some five million men (that is, just over 20 per cent of the adult male population) were in khaki, and the vast majority of them served overseas. They had to be equipped, fed and trained before being sent into the fighting. It is astonishing that this large-scale expansion took place without a major hiccup, and remains so little known about today. The one exception was the shell shortage of the spring and summer of 1915, which limited British offensive plans. In particular, the British campaign in Gallipoli and the Dardanelles was severely affected by this lack of munitions.

The structure of the army was fairly simple and logical, although the terminology may occasionally be confusing, and there were lots of exceptions. The paragraphs below give only a brief summary, but more detail is available on the Long Long Trail website.

In particular, the army used the word 'corps' in several different ways. Corps lay below 'armies' and above 'divisions' in the army command structure (see below). The specialist arms, such as the Royal Artillery and the Royal Engineers, were also formed into corps.

The campaign in the Dardanelles was the responsibility of the

Mediterranean Expeditionary Force (MEF). It was commanded first by General Sir Ian Hamilton, and then from mid-October by General Sir Charles Monro, who had previously commanded the Third Army in France. The MEF was composed of a Headquarters based on the Greek island of Lemnos, with various units attached as army troops. In turn Hamilton reported to Kitchener back in London.

As British forces arrived in theatre, VIII Corps was formed in May 1915, followed by IX Corps. In addition, of course, there was the Australian and New Zealand Army Corps (ANZAC). These corps replicated to an extent the structures of the armies above them. They too had units of army troops attached to their headquarters. And in turn they were responsible for several divisions.

In the case of VIII Corps, these divisions were the 29th (whose troops were among the first to land and the last to leave), the 42nd (East Lancashire), the 52nd (Lowland) and the Royal Naval Division (which was made up of sailors under military discipline). The IX Corps divisions comprised the 10th (Irish), 11th (Northern), 13th (Western), 53rd (Welsh), 54th (East Anglian) and 2nd Mounted. The three latter units arrived as reinforcements in August 1915. The ANZAC Corps comprised the 1st and 2nd Australian Divisions and the Australian and New Zealand Division, as well as some Indian units by August.

Divisions were the highest level echelons actively engaged in action. They were responsible for implementing the orders sent from corps and army headquarters. As a result, they were the most important units with which the ordinary soldier had any affinity. Each division included a number of infantry battalions and divisional troops made up of units of artillery, engineers and medical facilities. Very roughly, each division contained about 20,000 men. Below the divisions lay the brigades, each made up of two battalions and brigade troops.

The most important fighting unit was the infantry battalion, which at full strength consisted of about 1,000 men. Battalions belonged to a regiment. The regimental depot back in Britain was responsible for recruiting and training men (at least initially) and, through the wives of senior officers, organised support for men who had been taken prisoner of war and widows of those who had fallen.

From 1881 the regiments, with the exception of the Rifle Brigade and the King's Royal Rifle Corps, were linked to particular counties or cities. The affiliation is usually clear from the regimental title. In peacetime the regiment would recruit from the communities in the area, but of course men might choose to join a regiment other than their local one. Everybody at Gallipoli would have been a volunteer in one form or another, as conscription was not introduced until March 1916. Many men would have enlisted on the outbreak of war, or perhaps before the war they had been members of the Territorial Force or were reservists (that is, men who had already spent time in the army and were recalled to the colours on the outbreak of war).

In peacetime the regiment was made up of two battalions of regular soldiers, one of which was normally based in Great Britain or Ireland, while the other was overseas, generally in India. In addition, the 3rd and 4th Battalions were territorial or reservist units made up of part-time soldiers. On the outbreak of war there was a huge expansion of the army as men flocked to the colours. New infantry battalions were created almost on a daily basis. Some Territorial battalions were split to form cadres for new units. In some regiments these were simply sequentially numbered (typically 6th and 7th) but in others they were given a number which showed their ancestry – for example, the 5th King's Own was split into two battalions numbered 1/5th and 2/5th. Other battalions raised for the war were known as service battalions. These took their numbers immediately after the original Territorial battalions. The Hampshire Regiment, for example, eventually had nineteen battalions, of which the 2nd, a pre-war regular battalion, served in Gallipoli.

An infantry battalion was made up of battalion headquarters (BHQ) and four companies. The battalion was usually commanded by a lieutenant colonel, with a major as second in command. In addition, at BHQ would be the adjutant, who was in charge of battalion administration, including writing up the war diary; a quartermaster responsible for stores and transport; and a medical officer, on detachment from the Royal Army Medical Corps (RAMC). There you would also find the regimental sergeant-major (RSM), the most senior non-commissioned officer, plus a number of specialist roles filled by sergeants, including quartermasters, cooks, signallers and the orderly room clerk. There were also a number of specialist sections, such as signallers, machine gunners, drivers for the horse-drawn transport, and stretcher-bearers, who traditionally were the musicians of the battalion band.

As well as the Battalion HQ there were four companies, generally given the letters A to D. Each company was commanded by a major or a captain. In addition, there was a company sergeant-major (CSM) and the 'quarter bloke' – the company quartermaster sergeant (CQMS).

In turn companies were divided into four platoons, led by subalterns (junior officers), lieutenants and second lieutenants. Each platoon consisted of four sections, with each section generally comprising twelve men under an NCO. These were the men with whom an ordinary soldier would work, live and socialise. A private might also have dealings with the platoon commander and perhaps know the company and battalion commanders by sight.

More about the general organisation of the army can be found on the Long Long Trail website. In addition, Ray Westlake's *British Regiments at Gallipoli* (Pen & Sword, 2004) describes the contribution of each unit during the campaign.

The location of individual units is described in the Orders of Battle ('Orbats'), which offer a guide to the British Army based on its structure. They can be valuable because they list under which division, corps or army a battalion or unit served. What you won't find, however, is the physical location of individual units. The National Archives also has sets of Orders of Battle for the Mediterranean Expeditionary Force in WO 95/5473. Tim Travers includes detailed lists of units on the peninsula in April and August 1915 in *Gallipoli 1915* (Tempus, 2001).

However, you should not need to use them. Chris Baker's excellent Long Long Trail website contains increasing number of Orders of Battle arranged by echelon or by unit. Another useful shortcut is to look at the description of the battalion or unit war diary in the Discovery Catalogue on The National Archives website, which will give you the brigade and division that the battalion or unit was serving with, at least for part of its existence. In addition, this information is given in Ray Westlake's book.

Unit War Diaries

War diaries are the most important source in researching the activities of army units, whether they were in the front line or stationed a long way from the action. Official war diaries were introduced in 1908 and are still kept by units in action today.

War diaries were designed to record unit activities, particularly when it was in action. This, it was felt, would help analysis by historians and strategists so that they could learn lessons for future wars: they are very much the first draft of history. They were kept by infantry battalions and artillery batteries, as well as by higher echelons, such as brigades, divisions and even armies, as well as by more specialist units such as mobile hospitals, signals companies and field bakeries. With few exceptions, they survive only for units that served outside Britain and Ireland.

For researchers war diaries are the raw material of history because they contain the immediate records of each day's

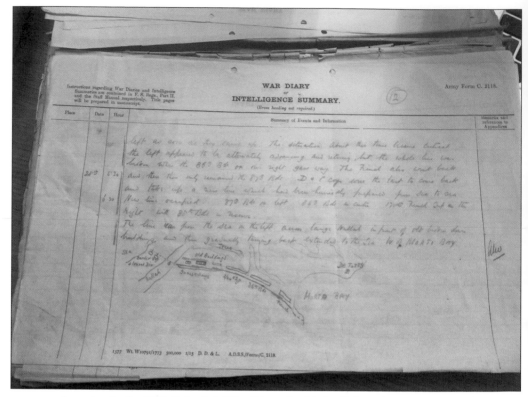

An entry in the 87th Brigade's War Diary for 28 April describing the events of the day, with a sketch map showing where the units were situated. War diaries are a key resource for the study of the Gallipoli Campaign. (TNA WO 95/4311)

activities unfiltered by further reflection and they sometimes contain the thoughts and feelings of the men compiling them (for some reason this seems to be particularly the case at Gallipoli). But, naturally, they are concerned only with what happened in their unit. To get the best from this source you need to use the diaries in conjunction with other records, such as published histories, memoirs and diaries, and official histories. It is a shame that they have not been more widely used by popular historians – Peter Hart, for example, does not quote from them in his otherwise magisterial account of the campaign. Perhaps this will change once they are all online.

War diaries were generally completed by the commanding officer, or in larger units by the adjutant, who otherwise was responsible for the general administration of the unit. Inevitably war diaries reflect the compiler's enthusiasm (or otherwise) for the task, but most are reasonably detailed, particularly when the unit was in the front line.

This is the entry for 10 August 1915 for the 5th Wiltshires, who were engaged in the desperate fight to defend the ridge at Chunuk Bair, as part of the attempted breakout from Anzac to join up with the new beachhead at Suvla Bay:

1a.m. (01.00) Battalion moved away in single file less D company and part of B company. Order of march C – Machine guns – A – B companies. The Battalion was guided, as far as I am able to ascertain, by a New Zealand officer. Here they arrived two hours before sunrise (circa 3.00) and the men were told to dig into dug outs and make themselves comfortable as the position was quite safe. Men therefore removed equipment and rifles. (Circa) 4.30 a.m. As soon as it was light machine guns opened on the men lying in their dug outs. About 1/4 of an hour later there was a rush of Turks from both sides of the depression which drove the men, unarmed and unequipped, down the gulley (SAZLI BEIT). The bottom of the gulley [was] commanded by machine guns and so escape was cut off. Three courses were possible: 1. To rush past the machine guns down the Sazli Beit; this was tried but in nearly all cases proved fatal. 2. To climb the northern slope of the ravine under fire and try to escape over the top. This was done in a few cases with success. 3. Hide in Gulley till night, this also was done with more success. Parties arrived on the Beach in fours, fives, and some carried bodies during the 11th, 12th and 13th unarmed, unequipped and demoralised. The Battalion when mustered on the Beach mustered roughly 420. (This includes 76 men lately arrived as Details from Lemnos.) Officer casualties: Lt Col. J. Carden (missing) 2nd Lieut J.E.R. Firmin (killed) 2nd Lt G. Gamman (missing) Maj. F. Ricketts (killed) 2nd Lieut W.Y. Radcliffe (killed) Lieut A.J. Hinxman (missing) Maj. W.S. Hern (killed) 2nd Lieut C.G.C. Fisher-Brown (missing) Capt & ADJ A.C. Belcher (killed) Lieut A.W. Huckett (missing) Lieut F.E. Hill (wounded) Lieut Brown (wounded – attached).

1a.m (0100) After the Battalion had marched off (A, C and part of B), D company under Major Hern relieved the Gurkhas with the Royal Irish Rifles in reserve. The position was attacked at dawn on Tuesday (10th) morning and through the retirement of the regiments on right and left. D company are left 'in the air'. Major Hern and Lieut J.E.R. Firmin killed but remainder hold on until surrounded and are forced to retire into Gulley. Here reorganised and sent up to a counter attack – unsuccessfully and with large loss. Lieut Gamman killed – several wanton attacks attempted with handfuls of men. At night men retire from Gulley, some taking refuge with 38th Bde. [www.thewardrobe. org.uk/research/war-diaries/detail/12857]

The Wiltshires had been attacked by a Turkish division led by Mustapha Kemal. The battalion was overrun, with half of the men never being seen again.

Peter Hart summarises the morning's events on the ridge:

The British plans had fallen into disarray . . . On Rhododendron Ridge and Chunuk Bair itself there were some 2,000 soldiers representing four different brigades and three different divisions. The New Zealanders had been relieved overnight and the Chunuk Bair positions were the responsibilities of the 6th Loyal North Lancashires and 5th Wiltshires. Many of the British soldiers were already exhausted, thirsty and demoralised . . . [The Turks] overwhelmed the British defenders before throwing themselves down the precipitous slopes in pursuit. [*Gallipoli*, p. 326]

Indeed, the 5th Wiltshires' war diary for the previous day records:

Heavy fighting was in progress in front, and the Battalion was shelled. Capt R.W.F. Jesson (wounded). During the day counter attacks by the Turks were expected but did not develop. Rations were drawn at 5.30p.m. and rumours were current of 24 hours rest. It should be noted that the men had had no rest, and very little water and food since Friday evening and were consequently in a very exhausted condition. [www.thewardrobe.org.uk/research/war-diaries /detail/12856]

Occasionally war diaries mention other, more peaceful activities. In the war diary for the 1/7th Cameronians for 21 July 1915, for example, there is this entry: 'Sea bathing did something to brighten the existence of the troops on the left flank, with the added novelty that the bathing frequently was interrupted by shell fire.' [WO 95/4321]

It is very unusual to find individual privates and non-commissioned officers mentioned, unless they had received an immediate gallantry award, and even then they might not appear. However, officers are generally mentioned, particularly those who were killed or wounded; less often individual officers are noted for the award of gallantry medals, when they were sent out to lead a patrol, or returned from leave.

As well as the diaries themselves, there may be accompanying appendices. These might consist of regimental orders, plans of attack, maps and other ephemeral information. Of particular interest are typewritten operational reports, which supplement entries in the war diaries themselves. Their survival is somewhat patchy.

It is important to remember that diaries were compiled by the battalion headquarters. Companies or sections may actually have been based some way away from the headquarters and their experiences might have been very different, but were not recorded. To an extent this is excusable in the chaos of battle. If you are lucky, you may be able to overcome this problem by using private papers, such as diaries, letters and memoirs.

War Diaries: Higher Echelons
In addition, there are war diaries for brigades, divisions and higher echelons. Inevitably, these contain less detail about day-to-day activities on the front, but more about the planning of battles and trench raids and meeting the logistical demands of tens of thousands of men. However, I have found copies of reports that are no longer with the battalion records. Certainly it is worth checking the brigade diaries, as these can give a more complete overview of what was actually going on in the trenches than a battalion war diary can.

In fact, for the higher echelons the term 'war diary' is rather a misnomer. The actual war diary is often no more than a page or two per month and may just record visits by senior officers and other inconsequential matters. The real meat lies in the accompanying appendices, which can include orders, reports, plans, maps and occasionally photographs. There is much material about the planning and preparation for battle.

There should be war diaries for each component part of divisions, corps and armies: that is, general staff (responsible for the planning and direction of the fighting), adjutant and quartermaster general (administration and supplying troops in the field), artillery, engineers and medical, as well as for those infantry and cavalry units attached to headquarters.

War Diaries: Their Location and Use

An almost complete set of diaries is at The National Archives in series WO 95 (with a few 'confidential war diaries' in WO 154, which generally mention individuals who appeared before courts martial). They are arranged by army, corps, division and brigade, although in practice this doesn't matter because it is easy to pick up individual units through the Discovery catalogue. The diaries are arranged by month and consist of entries in pencil on loose sheets of paper. Appendices tend to be typed or in the form of cyclostyle copies.

TNA has digitised the diaries for units that served only in France and Flanders. With the exception of the many ANZAC units and a few others, war diaries for units at Gallipoli still await digitisation. This means that you have to visit Kew to read the original diaries, which gives a curiously moving link with the men who compiled these diaries a hundred years ago.

Despite all the evidence to the contrary, TNA does not have a complete set, so if the unit diary appears to be missing it is worth approaching the regimental archives, as they often have duplicates. This is particularly the case with the Royal Artillery as TNA's holdings are rather patchy.

A few regimental museums have transcribed their war diaries and put them online, generally free of charge. For example, the Wardrobe Museum in Salisbury, which is the regimental museum for the Berkshire and Wiltshire Regiments, has done so for its battalion war diaries for both world wars.

REGIMENTAL HISTORIES

Any regiment worth its name will have had several histories written about it. The earliest were published in the mid-nineteenth century and examples are still being written today.

Most regiments and service corps have specific histories relating to the unit during the First World War. Inevitably they vary greatly in quality and interest. The best include interviews with former officers or copies of letters they wrote home describing incidents and battles, but most simply offer a workmanlike overview of what each battalion did, theatre by theatre and month by month. Although they are now rather dated, serious researchers should not ignore them.

Also worth looking out for are the divisional histories, which describe the war from the perspective of the division HQ. Histories of the 11th, 29th, 42nd, 52nd and Royal Naval Divisions have been reprinted by the Naval & Military Press.

There is a detailed bibliography arranged by regiment and arm available on the Army Museums Ogilby Trust website (www.armymuseums.org.uk).

The Imperial War Museum and the National Army Museum have major collections, while The National Archives and the Society of Genealogists library also contain useful collections. Regimental museums and local libraries should have regimental diaries for units raised in their area. Many such histories have been republished by the Military & Naval Press.

Since the 1970s there has been an explosion of unofficial battalion histories, such as the series about the Pals battalions for Pen & Sword, describing the activities of individual units. Most are meticulously researched and illustrated and are well worth consulting.

TRENCH MAPS

From early 1915 British surveyors and mapmakers began to map the trenches using sketches drawn by observers in aircraft. They were particularly needed in Gallipoli, in part because of the almost non-existent pre-war mapping but also because of the difficult terrain.

During the eight months of the campaign a varied range of

different maps were drawn up, but they are typically not as thorough or accurate as their Western Front equivalents. The Western Front Association has published some 300 maps on the DVD *Gallipoli: Mapping the Front*. As well as maps, there are photographic panoramas of Gallipoli that were used by the artillery. Details are available at www.westernfrontassociation. com/great-war-mapping/mapping-the-front-great-war-maps-dvd/ great-war-map-lists/860-maplist-gallipoli.html. They are based on maps at TNA in series WO 301. In addition, there are a few maps in WO 153, and unit war diaries often contain copies of maps showing trench systems in their sectors.

Copies can also be found at the Imperial War Museum. The National Army Museum, Royal Naval Museum and regimental museums may also have copies.

Further Reading
Peter Chasseaud (with Peter Doyle), *Grasping Gallipoli – Terrain, Maps and Failure at the Dardanelles* (Spellmount, 2005) and *Mapping the First World War: The Great War through maps from 1914–1918* (Imperial War Museum, 2013).

Official Histories
During the 1920s the government commissioned historians to prepare detailed official histories of the war, formally known as the History of the Great War based on Official Documents. The intention was to learn lessons, both tactical and logistic, from the war and also to provide an authoritative historical account. Historians have often dismissed official histories as mere propaganda – 'official but not history', in the military historian Basil Liddell Hart's tart phrase. But they are worth consulting, if for no other reason than that they contain some superb maps of the battlefields. However, they are likely to be hard going for the novice, as the official histories can be quite technical.

Official histories for the Gallipoli Campaign are *Gallipoli. Vol. I: Inception of the Campaign to May 1915*, compiled by Brigadier General C.F. Aspinall-Oglander (London: William Heinemann, 1929), with a separate volume of appendices, and *Gallipoli. Vol. II: May 1915 to the Evacuation*, compiled by C.F. Aspinall-Oglander (London: William Heinemann, 1932), with a separate volume of appendices. In addition, both the Australian and New Zealand governments also commissioned official histories: C.E.W. Bean, *The Story of ANZAC* (2 vols, 1921) and Fred Waite, *The New Zealanders at Gallipoli* (1921).

Two semi-official accounts are Sir Ian Hamilton's *Despatches from the Dardanelles* and Sir Ian Hamilton's *Final Despatch from the Dardanelles* (1916). Hamilton's *Gallipoli Diary* (1920) and Henry Nevinson's *The Dardanelles Campaign* (1918) are other contemporary works worth looking out for.

With the exception of Bean's Story of ANZAC and Hamilton's Diary, reprints of the other books are available from the Naval & Military Press and most can also be downloaded free of charge from the Internet Archive (www.archive.org).

Before the histories were published, drafts were sent to officers who had fought in the campaign for their comments. Their replies can be very informative and offer honest insights into how battles were viewed by officers, although inevitably their opinions often contain more than a hint of hindsight. Major B.G. Weller of the Royal Marines commented on a paragraph describing the exhaustion of the RM Light Infantry's Plymouth Battalion in July 1915:

. . . the reason for the exhaustion was chiefly because of dysentery. In the Plymouth Bn [Battalion] . . . scarcely an officer or man was immune and it was the same in the other Bns. Sheer physical weakness from dysentery was at the root of everything. Further, men who had been up all night in the front line or those in rear who were digging at night (as happened with the utmost frequency) could get no sleep by day owing to the plague of flies which swarmed over everyone and everything . . . [CAB 45/245 with copy in WO 95/4291]

The correspondence, together with a small collection of private diaries and related paperwork, including several enemy accounts, is at The National Archives in series CAB 45/215–261. You may also come across copies in the war diaries themselves (as with the example of Major Weller above).

OFFICIAL DESPATCHES

After each war or campaign, commanders-in-chief are expected to summarise the successes and failures in a despatch that is then published in the *London Gazette*. The ones for the First World War are surprisingly readable. Sir Ian Hamilton, the commander of the British forces for most of the Gallipoli Campaign, was a published poet and an engaging writer. In the despatches they traditionally mention service personnel of all ranks worthy of special praise, hence the term 'Mention in Despatches' (sometimes abbreviated to MID). The Official Despatches are now rarely used by historians, but might be of interest, particularly if your ancestor was one of the men and women who were mentioned in despatches. It is rare, however, to find why an individual was so commemorated.

The despatches are available online through the *London Gazette* website (www.thegazette.co.uk), but it is probably easier to read the texts on the Long Long Trail website at www.1914-1918.net/Gallipoli.htm, although Chris Baker does not include any of the lists of names which accompanied the original despatches. Sir Ian Hamilton wrote three despatches, which were published in 1916.

THE DARDANELLES COMMISSION

A Royal Commission was set up in July 1916 to investigate the failures of the Dardanelles Campaign and eventually issued an anodyne report in 1919. It was, as *The Times* said, to be 'a study in surrender'. Members interviewed most of the major protagonists, particularly Sir Ian Hamilton, so if you are looking at a particular commander or action there may be something useful here. The records of the Commission are largely in series CAB 19, with the conclusion online at www.nationalarchives. gov.uk/pathways/firstworldwar/battles/p_dard_comm.htm.

PHOTOGRAPHS AND FILM

By far the largest collection of First World War-related material is at the Imperial War Museum. At the heart of the Museum's collections are some 40,000 official photographs showing all aspects of the war. As it took time for a satisfactory system to be set up, and particularly to overcome suspicion from the military authorities, the photographic record is more comprehensive from mid-1916 onwards than it is for the first half of the war, so there is relatively little for Gallipoli. Initially a number of soldiers took cameras with them to the battlefields, but cameras were banned in the spring of 1915. The Australian authorities took a much more relaxed attitude to photography, so there are major collections of material at the Australian War Memorial in Canberra. This collection is supplemented by material donated by individual servicemen. Many images, but certainly not all, are described in the online catalogue at www.iwm.org.uk/ collections/search.

Regimental Museums and local studies libraries may also have collections of material. For example, the Suffolk Regiment Archive at Suffolk Record Office in Bury St Edmunds has an album of photographs taken by Lieutenant B.W. Cockell of the 5th Battalion, and loose photographs donated by CSM C. Smith MM. In addition, TNA has a small collection of photographs in series WO 317.

The Imperial War Museum's Film and Video Archive has by far

the largest collection of films. The collection is described in Roger Smithers (ed.), *The Imperial War Museum Film Catalogue Volume 1: The First World War* (Flick Books, 1997). One or two films are now online, notably the 1916 Australian production Heroes of Gallipoli, which lasts about twenty minutes (www.iwm.org.uk/ collections/item/object/1060023379).

Also worth checking out are newsreels – short news stories shown at local cinemas. Those for the First World War largely concentrate on the 'home front'. There is a list at http://bufvc. ac.uk/newsonscreen/search. British Pathe (www.britishpathe. com) and Movietone (www.movietone.com) have clips from their newsreels available on their websites free of charge. Unfortunately there is almost nothing about the Dardanelles or Gallipoli, **although** there are several short films (and longer features) on YouTube.

WAR DIARY, 2ND BATTALION, SOUTH WALES BORDERERS, 24–5 APRIL 1915

The 2nd Battalion landed on S Beach, which was captured without much effort. Without further orders they did not advance as perhaps they should have to take advantage of Turkish weakness. It is thought now that there was no more than a platoon or two of enemy soldiers on or near the beach.

24 April
5pm – Received order to go on board HMS *Cornwallis*. 4 trawlers came alongside SS *Alannia* to take Battalion Office. 7.3pm – All battalion embarked except 6 sick, 4 staff sergeants and 4 storemen.

25 April
4.30am – Stood by ready to get into the trawler. *Cornwallis* signals to trawlers to come aside about 5am. Men rapidly

change into trawlers and *Cornwallis* steams slowly in towards MORTO BAY . . .

7am – *Cornwallis* makes signal for men to enter small boats

7.30am – Landing effected as follows: trawlers in succession steam in towards shore, on getting in as close as possible a stern anchor was thrown out and small boats cast away. These boats row for the shore as quickly as possible.

D Company first to land made for DE TOTTS Battery at once. C & B companies on landing made the trench in front of beach at range of about 100 yards. Manoeuvre completely successful. D Company cleared DE TOTTS and B and C Companies took trench with the bayonet capturing about 15 Turks.

8.30am – Our position secured. D Company on DE TOTTS Battery and B and C Companies on a ridge about 400 yards North North West. Some Marines from *Cornwallis* land with us to assist with the boats, these men did excellent work.

Our casualties were not heavy considering the position we attacked. Had it been held by resolute men we should never have been able to capture it without some loss.

Casualties – Officers Major G C Margesson and Lieutenant R P Behrens killed. Captain D G Johnson, G H Birkitt and Lt W J Chamberlain wounded. Other ranks killed 12, wounded 40, missing 6.

9am – Watched the landing at SEDD-EL-BAHR. This however did not appear to be a success. We could see troops trying to work up through the ruined village but without success.

10am – Troops observed moving from X Beach moving East. This attack however appeared to be diverted towards SEDD-EL-BAHR. From this fact we gathered that the landing at SEDD-EL-BAHR had failed and we were quite isolated. Steps at once taken to consolidate our position, especially as prisoners informed us that 2000 Turks were in our vicinity.

Position taken up, D Company and half a platoon C Company in DE TOTTS Battery. Three platoons B Company and half a platoon C Company in small raids North East of landing place with 3 platoons C Company and 1 platoon B Company and Royal Engineer Detachment in support.

Field hospital detachment with Naval detachment remained in trees just beneath DE TOTTS where there was excellent supply of water. Guns from KUM KHALE continually shelled our position but without much damage . . .

Our orders were to push on towards North North West (NNW) and join up with our Brigade, but in view of the state of affairs the Commanding Officer decided to remain where he was.

12.20pm – General situation appeared very involved.

Troops appeared to be moving towards Hills 138 and 114 and Turks retiring from 114 were heavily shelled by [HMS] *Queen Elizabeth* and *Cornwallis*.

2pm – Message received: 'On W and Y Beaches landing is progressing favourably but on V Beach attack is held up by wire – Australians doing well.'

11pm – Alarm given and a great deal of firing took place at our position; we did not fire much, a few rounds now and then when anyone came close.

This extract was taken from the Unit War Diary in WO 95/4311 at The National Archives. For more about the South Wales Borderers on S Beach there is a useful essay by Peter Hart at http://archive.iwm.org.uk/upload/package/2/gallipoli /pdf_files/SBeach.pdf.

Chapter 6

THE ROYAL NAVY

The Royal Navy played a major, if now almost forgotten, role in the Dardanelles campaign. Initially it was hoped that bombarding the Turkish forces and passing through The Narrows between Europe and Asia Minor towards the Sea of Marmara and Constantinople would have forced a Turkish surrender. Had the navy been successful in taking control of the seas in February and March, the Gallipoli invasion might not have taken place. But this was not to be. Instead, naval ships continued to play a key role in landing troops, evacuating the wounded, bombarding Turkish positions and protecting the peninsula from attack by enemy naval forces. But the Dardanelles exposed the weaknesses of the big ships, which were vulnerable to attack by enemy submarines – on 13 May HMS *Goliath* was sunk by a Turkish torpedo boat, with the loss of 570 lives, and a fortnight later, on 27 May, HMS *Majestic* was sunk by the German submarine U-21 with 700 casualties – or in danger of blundering into unknown minefields, as happened on 18 March when three battle-cruisers were lost. The big capital ships were withdrawn to safer anchorages and thereafter made only infrequent visits. This not unnaturally caused the troops, who had become used to seeing the ships on the horizon, to feel that they had been abandoned in some way.

Naval aircraft conducted aerial reconnaissance over the area, while submarines probed the Narrows and sank a number of Turkish merchant ships. In addition, sailors from the Royal Naval Division fought alongside their army colleagues in many of the battles, although its most famous member, the poet Rupert Brooke, died of acute blood poisoning a few days before the landings.

The naval operations were the responsibility of two men. Rear Admiral Michael De Robeck, commanding the Eastern Mediterranean Squadron, directed naval operations. He reported to Rear Admiral Rosslyn Wemyss, the Senior Naval Officer on Lemnos. According to James Goldrick's biography in the Oxford Dictionary of National Biography:

> Wemyss soon encountered all the confusion which marked the early operations against Turkey. Lemnos was Greek and thus neutral, but Wemyss was expected to act as governor and senior naval officer with no formal instructions and no legal authority. More critically, he had no depot ships, little physical plant, and very few administrative staff to organize a base. Wemyss succeeded in matching conflicting service and national priorities with his necessarily hand-to-mouth organization by relying almost wholly on his personal influence. Mudros proved a miracle of improvisation and the ability of the allies to sustain the long Dardanelles campaign of 1915–16 depended very largely upon it.

UNIT RECORDS

It can be frustratingly difficult to track down reports and descriptions of naval activities during the First World War. No records are yet online and the cataloguing of the records leaves a lot to be desired. The logs of individual ships, which are in series ADM 53, normally include only weather and navigational details. Perhaps of more immediate use are the ships' histories at www.battleships-cruisers.co.uk/royal.htm. In addition, brief histories can generally be found on Wikipedia.

Detailed reports of operations (including reports from individual ship's captains), plans, drawings of the beaches, signals, recommendations for honours and awards and so on are mainly in series ADM 137. There are some forty volumes under the heading of Dardanelles alone, but it is also worth trying series ADM 1 and ADM 116 as well. There is quite a lot of duplication, but if you are prepared to wade through the volumes you will be able to build up a very good picture of naval operations around Gallipoli. Fortunately, many individual volumes are indexed, so they are easy to go through. The private papers of both De Robeck and Wemyss relating to the Dardanelles Campaign are at Churchill College, Cambridge. There is also likely to be some material at the Royal Naval Museum in Portsmouth (www.royalnavalmuseum.org/ research.htm) and at the Royal Marines Museum and the Royal Navy Submarine Museum, both also in the Portsmouth area. In addition, a few charts of the area are in ADM 344. War diaries for the Royal Naval Division and its brigades are in WO 95 and ADM 137.

However, any study of the naval side of Gallipoli should begin with the official history. The Naval History Net website has made available Sir Julian Corbett's official history, which was published in 1921. Although dated, it is still the best place to start in order to understand the role that the navy played. Individual ships and senior officers may be mentioned, but it is rare to find mention of junior officers or ratings. The Naval & Military Press has also republished the Royal Naval Division's official history by Douglas Jerrold.

There was little formal air activity over Gallipoli. Royal Naval Air Service aircraft flew aerial reconnaissance and artillery spotting missions and launched occasional raids on Turkish fortifications from ships positioned in the Dardanelles. There are a dozen files in the AIR 1 series that might be useful. There is also an interesting article by Peter Hart on the air war at http://archive.iwm.org.uk/upload/package/2/gallipoli/pdf_files/ GallipoliAirWar.pdf and another by Raul Colon at www.century-of-flight.net/Aviation%20history/airplane%20at%20war/turk.htm

PERSONNEL RECORDS

Unless indicated otherwise, the records described here can be downloaded (for a fee: currently £3.30 per document) from The National Archives Online Records Service. Service records for men who were in the navy after the mid-1920s are with the Ministry of Defence. You can find details at www.veterans-uk.info.

THE ROYAL NAVY

Commissioned Officers and Warrant Officers

Brief details of officers' postings and ranks can be found in published Navy Lists. You are likely to be able to get an idea of when they entered, the branch they were in, subsequent promotions and the ship they were serving on at the time the List was published. A set of Navy Lists can be found online at www.archive.org, although they are not easy to use. Promotions and resignations are also included in the *London Gazette*, which is online at www.thegazette.co.uk.

Service records for officers and non-commissioned warrant officers who served during the war are in ADM 196. You should find details of the officer's family and his date of birth, promotions and ships served on, together with brief notes about his performance. Another useful resource is the summaries of confidential reports (also in ADM 196) containing candid comments written by senior officers on an individual's abilities. Also worth checking are the record cards and files in ADM 340.

Ratings and Petty Officers

Records of ratings are in series ADM 188. They can tell you the ships a man served on, any medals won, promotions and remarks about conduct, and an indication of how and when he left the navy. Incidentally, the abbreviation DD means 'discharged dead', while the word 'run' indicates that he deserted. Generally the forms are easy to read.

THE ROYAL NAVAL RESERVE AND THE ROYAL NAVAL VOLUNTEER RESERVE

As well as the regular navy, there were also the Royal Naval Reserve (RNR), recruited from merchant seamen, and the larger Royal Naval Volunteer Reserve (RNVR), previously yachtsmen or members of the general public. Again officers are listed in the Navy Lists and the *London Gazette*. Service records for officers and other ranks in both Reserves are easy to use, although their content is rather brief.

The Royal Naval Reserve (RNR)

At the outbreak of the First World War the RNR had a strength of around 30,000 men.

Officers are listed in the Navy Lists, where information given includes name, rank, date of commission and seniority, as well as the ships on which the officers served. Service records up to 1920 are in ADM 240. They are arranged by rank and seniority, show details of merchant as well as naval service, and are arranged in numerical order of commission. Additional information can often be found in the service cards and files in ADM 340.

Records of RNR Ratings between 1914 and 1919 are available in ADM 337 with additional records in BT 377.

The Royal Naval Volunteer Reserve (RNVR)

The Royal Naval Volunteer Reserve (RNVR), founded in 1903, comprised officers and ratings who undertook naval training in their spare time but were not professional seamen. Officers are listed in the Navy Lists. Service records of RNVR officers can be found in two series: ADM 337 and occasionally ADM 340. Service records for ratings are also in ADM 337. They record when a man joined, which ships he served on and his reasons for leaving the Reserve. There is also a physical description.

THE ROYAL NAVAL DIVISION

The Royal Naval Division (RND) was initially set up to make use of reservists for whom there were no places on board ships, although most members were recruits who preferred to enlist in the navy than the army. They served at Gallipoli and then in Flanders and eventually transferred to the army in 1916 as the 63rd (Royal Naval) Division. Individual brigades were named after naval heroes. Even on land the RND retained many naval traditions, much to the annoyance of the army high command. They flew the White Ensign, used bells to signal time, used naval language (including 'going ashore' and 'coming on board' for leaving and arriving in the trenches), preferred naval ranks to their army equivalents and sat during the toast to the king's health. Attempts were made to persuade the RND to conform with army practice but were generally unsuccessful.

Service records for officers in the Royal Naval Division (RND) are in ADM 339/3, with the equivalent for ratings in ADM 339/1, although the records for ratings who died on active service are in ADM 339/2.

The service records can be fairly informative, particularly for officers and for men killed in action. In all cases they give details of next of kin, date of birth, address, religion and civilian occupation, together with a physical description. Within the division the card records movements and postings and, where appropriate, a date of death. For men who died in service, the information is largely summarised in databases of the division's casualties, which are on both Ancestry and Findmypast.

ROYAL MARINES

During the First World War the Royal Marines were divided into RM Light Infantry and RM Artillery. Both served on land (as part of the Royal Naval Division) and at sea. Royal Marine officers' records (including warrant officers) are in series ADM 196. They give full details of service and include, in some cases, the name and profession of the officer's father. Officers are also listed in both the Navy and Army Lists.

Service records for Marines are in ADM 159. They provide date and place of birth, trade, physical description, religion, date and place of enlistment, and a full record of service with comments on conduct. In addition, there are attestation papers in ADM 157, which are loose forms, compiled for each Marine on enlistment. They give birthplace, previous occupation, a physical description and often a record of service.

Many service records for men who served in the Chatham, Deal and Plymouth Divisions (but not Portsmouth) during the First World War are at the Fleet Air Arm Museum at Yeovilton (www.fleetairarm.com/naval-aviation-research.aspx).

Awards of campaign and gallantry medals are in the Naval Medal Records series, online through Ancestry. Perhaps of more use are the transcriptions of the Cards for the Marines on Findmypast. Marine casualties are listed alphabetically in series ADM 242/7–10 (and on Findmypast), giving name, rank, number, ship's name, date and place of birth, cause of death, where buried and next-of-kin. Some war diaries for Marine units serving with the army are in WO 95. In addition, some material is held at the Royal Marines Museum in Southsea: www.royalmarinesmuseum. co.uk.

MEDALS

Naval personnel were entitled to the same campaign medals as their army counterparts. Rolls are available through Ancestry, although they are much less informative than the Army Medal Index Cards. A full list of men who received gallantry medals, taken from entries in the *London Gazette*, can be found at http://naval-history.net. Reports from captains about individual actions or other occurrences often include recommendations for gallantry medals.

CASUALTIES

Sailors who died during their naval service are commemorated by the Commonwealth War Graves Commission in exactly the same way as soldiers or airmen. Officers and ratings with no known graves, including men who were lost at sea around Gallipoli, are commemorated on memorials at Chatham, Portsmouth and Plymouth.

Details of some 45,000 Royal Navy and Royal Marine officers and ratings who died during the First World War are listed in the War Graves Roll in ADM 242. The roll gives full name, rank, service number, ship's name, date and place of birth, cause of death, where buried and next of kin. The records are on Findmypast. Further registers of killed and wounded are in ADM 104/145–6.

Both Ancestry and Findmypast have databases of the casualties of the Royal Naval Division. There is an online list of naval casualties at http://naval-history.net which can be searched by name or by ship. Entries are quite detailed, giving the man's name, rank and ship, together with the date of death and occasionally the cause of death.

Often captains' (and other) reports into actions involving naval ships will include lists of casualties; these reports appear in series ADM 137, ADM 116 and ADM 1. Generally they just give the deceased's name, rank, trade and next of kin, but the reports themselves may indicate how he lost his life. These reports are not online.

Further Reading

Three excellent websites are www.worldwar1.co.uk, www.uboat.net/wwi and www.naval-history.net.

The most up-to-date guide to researching sailors is Simon Fowler, *Tracing Your Naval Ancestors* (Pen & Sword, 2011).

Chapter 7

RESEARCHING DOMINION AND INDIAN TROOPS

Gallipoli was a particularly international campaign. On the Allied side were British soldiers from the four corners of the British Isles, Australians, Gurkhas, New Zealanders, Newfoundlanders and Sikhs. With the French served Algerians and Senegalese. And on the Turkish side were Turks and men from across the Ottoman Empire, as well as Germans and Austrians. All of them were engaged in bitter fighting over a few square miles of mountainous scrubland.

When Britain declared war on 4 August 1914 she did so on behalf of the Empire as well as the United Kingdom itself. The five dominions – Australia, Canada, Newfoundland, New Zealand and South Africa – were self-governing, but generally left their defence and foreign affairs to the British government. In part this reflected the belief in most people's minds that they were as British as any Londoner, Yorkshireman or Glaswegian. So it was natural that when the call came the dominions would not be found wanting.

The landings of the Australian and New Zealand troops at what became known as Anzac Cove on 25 April 1915 changed the relationship between these dominions and the Mother Country for ever and rapidly led to a burgeoning sense of national identity on both sides of the Tasman Sea. The myth is so powerful that the tendency is to forget that the Anzacs made up only a relatively small part of the Allied forces on the peninsula, and

117

Anzac soldiers using trench periscopes to keep an eye on the Turks across no man's land.

their contribution, great though it was, was part of a wider effort. And it is important to remember that Anzacs came from two distinct nations, a distinction subtly reinforced by the New Zealanders' inclusion of the simple inscription on the base of their memorials 'From the uttermost ends of the earth'. Individual diggers and kiwis had subtly different personalities. According to Lieutenant Colonel M.E. Hamilton, 'The Australian fighter was an individualist. He would go off and fight his own battle in his own way. And he didn't take very kindly to discipline . . . [The New Zealanders were] equally brave, equally tough soldiers. But you could talk to a New Zealander almost as you would to English people . . . You didn't have the same rapport with the Australians who were a rougher diamond.'

No Canadian (or South African) units were at Gallipoli, but the Newfoundland Regiment served as part of the 88th Brigade.

There was also the semi-autonomous Indian Empire based in New Delhi, which maintained the Indian Army, under the direct control of the Viceroy. It was largely led by British officers, with native troops as ordinary soldiers and non-commissioned officers. A number of Sikh and Gurkha units fought at Gallipoli. Their contributions have perhaps not been sufficiently recognised by historians, but at times they played a key role. Major Cecil Allanson of the 1/6th Gurkha Rifles wrote in his memoirs that in the battle for Hill Q on the morning of 9 August his men 'fought hand to hand, we bit and fisted, and used rifles and pistols as clubs; blood was flying about like spray from a hair-wash bottle. And then the Turks turned and fled, and I felt a very proud man . . .'.

In general the records for dominion and Indian servicemen are very similar to those used for researching British servicemen or British army units. Indeed, there are some shared records:

• The Commonwealth War Graves Commission records the last resting place of all Dominion and Indian troops;
• Gallantry awards for all ranks, and the commissions and promotion of officers in Dominion forces, appear in the London Gazette; and
• Copies of the war diaries of many ANZAC units are at The National Archives, although the quality of the copying is poor.

AUSTRALIA

The National Archives of Australia holds service documents for, among other formations, the 1st Australian Imperial Force (AIF), the Australian Flying Corps, and the Australian Army Nursing Service, and has Depot or home records for personnel who served within Australia. The records are at www.naa.gov.au/collection/explore/defence/service-records/army-wwi.aspx. Also of interest is the AIF Project, which lists the details of those who served overseas with the Australian Imperial Force (www.aif.adfa.edu.au).

The Australian War Memorial (www.awm.gov.au) has a superb collection of material relating to Australian forces since 1901. Many records have been indexed or digitised, and placed online free of charge. You can find details at www.awm.gov.au/collection/digitised-record.

They include:

• A roll of honour with some personnel details;
• a First World War Embarkation Roll which contains details of approximately 330,000 AIF personnel as they left on overseas service;
• a First World War Nominal Roll with details of 324,000 AIF personnel who served overseas;
• honours and awards, with details of recommendations, made to members of the AIF;

- war diaries compiled by Australian units; and
- official histories commissioned by the Australian government.

Through the Anzac Collections programme the Memorial is digitising the personal papers and diaries of 150 Anzacs. Details are at www.awm.gov.au/1914-1918/anzac-connections. One of the most poignant diaries is that of Private Cecil McNaulty of the 1st Australian Infantry Brigade. He kept it from the time he left Australia until 6 August 1915, when he was one of the nearly two thousand men of the brigade to charge the Turkish trenches at Lone Pine. In what he described as being a trance-like state, Cecil pushed through the heavy machine gun and rifle fire with shrapnel shells bursting around him. Having advanced to the Turkish lines, he found himself in an extremely exposed position along with several other Australians. 'This is only suicide, boys,' Cecil told them. 'I'm going to make a jump for it.' Cecil's account of what happened next ends mid-sentence with the words: 'I sprang to my feet in one jump . . .'. There are no further entries. But official records show that he was not killed then, but died a few days later.

Also available are the papers of General John Monash. By profession a civil engineer, Monash became one of the war's outstanding commanders. His papers give a comprehensive view of his wartime military career, from his command of the 4th Australian Brigade at Gallipoli to the Australian Corps in 1918.

If you are ever in Canberra, the Australian War Memorial is definitely well worth visiting.

The National Library of Australia's Trove website (www.trove. nla.gov.au) is a brilliant resource with digitised newspapers, books, photographs and personal papers. As might be expected, there is a lot of material about the Dardanelles, including newspaper reports, contemporary books and photographs.

There are also a number of excellent websites devoted to the

Anzacs. Start with www.anzacsite.gov.au, which is an impressively well written and well researched site devoted to the Anzac involvement in the campaign. The Australian War Memorial (www.awm.org.au) has masses of information about the Australian (and to an extent New Zealand) involvement at Gallipoli, although it is not always easy to find. For New Zealanders there is the slightly disappointing Anzac Day website (www.anzac.govt.nz).

Another useful site is the Australian Light Horse Study Centre (http://alh-research.tripod.com/Light_Horse/index.blog?topic_id =1113739), which has many copies of original reports and other documents including war diaries.

Official histories prepared by both the Australian and New Zealand governments in the early 1920s can be downloaded from the Internet Archive free of charge. There are links on the Gallipoli Association website at www.gallipoli-association.org.

New Zealand

Personnel records of nearly 120,000 men who served in the New Zealand Expeditionary Force and were discharged before the end of 1920 are held by Archives New Zealand and can be downloaded at http://archway.archives.govt.nz. In addition, the Archives also has nominal and casualty rolls, rolls of honour, unit (war) diaries and records relating to honours and awards, which are briefly described in a research guide at http://archives.govt.nz/research/guides/war#first. Unfortunately these records are not yet online.

Auckland War Memorial Museum's Cenotaph Database at http://muse.aucklandmuseum.com/databases/cenotaph has brief details about most New Zealand troops, particularly those who did not return. The Database is being redeveloped for the centenary.

The National Library of New Zealand has digitised many of the country's newspapers, which are now available through the excellent Papers Past website (http://paperspast.natlib.govt.nz). As might be expected, there is a lot about the Dardanelles campaign from the moment the first New Zealanders landed up to the present day.

The Library also has a very good introductory leaflet explaining how to research the war, with links to key resources and archives (http://natlib.govt.nz/researchers/guides/first-world-war), as well as to those of the Library's own collections that have already been digitised. This includes several collections of photographs.

INDIA

The location of the service records of Indian privates and non-commissioned officers is not known. A few medal index cards survive, generally for men who served in colonial campaigns that took place in 1918 and 1919. These are available on both The National Archives website and Ancestry. The remainder of the cards are presumed to have long since been destroyed.

Records for British officers in the Indian Army are at the British Library in London (www.bl.uk). Unfortunately, there are many different, and at times duplicating, sources, which can make research difficult. Perhaps the best place to start is with an online database (http://indiafamily.bl.uk/UI) of British civil and military employees living in India, but it is by no means complete.

Service records for officers and warrant officers are in series IOL L/MIL/14. Some indexes are online at www.nationalarchives.gov.uk/a2a. However, it may be easier to use the British Library's catalogue to its own Archives and Manuscripts at http://search archives.bl.uk.

War diaries for many Indian units that served at Gallipoli are in series WO 95 at Kew.

Further Reading
Emma Jolly, *Tracing Your British Indian Ancestors* (Pen & Sword, 2010).

NEWFOUNDLAND

The Newfoundland Regiment was at Gallipoli between 20 September 1915 and 9 January 1916. Library and Archives Canada holds many records for men and women who served in the Canadian and Newfoundland forces during the First World War at Collections Canada portal (www.collectionscanada.ca). Unfortunately, the databases are not always easy to use and the information available is partial, but there is help at www.collectionscanada.gc.ca/genealogy/022-909.006-e.html.

Surviving service records of the Newfoundland Regiment are online at www.therooms.ca/regiment/part3_database.asp. War diaries are at The National Archives in Kew in WO 95/4312. There is also a website devoted to the history of the Newfoundland Regiment, with more about the part it played at Gallipoli: www.rnfldr.ca/history.aspx?item=41.

Chapter 8

VISITING GALLIPOLI

Almost since the end of the First World War the battlefields of Gallipoli have been attracting tourists, although for decades visitors were few in number, put off by its remoteness and inaccessibility. Alan Moorhead, the first modern historian of the campaign, observed:

> The cemeteries at Gallipoli are unlike those of any other battlefield in Europe . . . There is no sound except for the wind in the trees and the calls of the migrating birds who have in these places the safest sanctuary on the peninsula . . . Often for months at a time nothing of any consequence happens, lizards scuttle about the tombstones in the sunshine and time goes by in an endless dream.

Since the 1980s this has changed as Turkey has modernised. Modern roads were built into the area and there has been considerable development, mostly for the better, with many new hotels and restaurants. If possible, you should try to visit Gallipoli and the Dardanelles to see the battlefields and the cemeteries. Without doing so, it is almost impossible to visualise the battles and the sacrifices made by the men of both sides.

Organised Tours
Many visitors prefer organised tours where everything is provided, and they are probably worth it if you are either nervous about organising your own tour or want to explore the area thoroughly. There are, however, far fewer tours than to the

Western Front and they sell out quickly. Listed below are five companies that organise one or more trips a year from Britain to the area, but no doubt there are others. The Gallipoli Association (www.gallipoli-association.org) also runs a couple of tours a year for members.

- Battlefield Breaks – http://battlefield-breaks.com
- Battle Honours – www.battle-honours.eu
- Holts Tours – http://holts.co.uk
- Leger Holidays – www.visitbattlefields.co.uk
- Spirit of Remembrance – www.spiritofremembrance.com

To get the most out of your trip, make sure that the tour is led by a member of the Guild of Battlefield Guides, as these guides are extremely knowledgeable and are used to dealing with groups.

It is possible to do day trips to Gallipoli from Istanbul. If you are visiting the city on holiday and your time is short, such a trip may be worth considering, but inevitably you will only get the broadest of overviews. TripAdvisor members recommend Gallipoli Tour (www.gallipolitour.com), which offers two-day tours, and RSL Tours (www.rsltours.com). Again no doubt there are other companies in the field but you should try to check them out before booking.

If you stay in Çanakkale, across from Gallipoli on the Asian side of the Straits, then there are also several companies which offer day tours, including Lutars Travel (www.gallipoliexperience.com/en).

Self-Guided Tours

If you are comfortable with driving in Turkey, you might wish to hire a car in Istanbul and drive down to the peninsula. The D3 motorway west from Istanbul speeds up the journey somewhat. The advantages are that you get to go to the places you want to go to, and can take as long about it as you like. (One disadvantage with organised tours – particular the short one- or two-day ones – is that they have a tendency just to visit the cemeteries.)

According to Nigel Steel, the best time to visit is in the early summer – late April, May and early June – when it is not too hot but the ground is firm enough to walk across with ease. Even so, you will need a stout pair of boots and trousers capable of resisting prickly pear thorns. As the soldiers, of course, found during the summer of 1915, it can be fearsomely hot in the sun so it is important to take adequate supplies of water and sun cream.

In Peter Hart's history of the campaign, *Gallipoli* (2011), he suggests a three-day itinerary, based on staying in Eceabat or Çanakkale. There is also an interesting article by Geoff Moran about visiting the peninsula by car at www.hellfirecorner.co.uk/moran/morangallip.htm.

There are a few walking routes, but because of the terrain they are not suitable for novices. The official Anzac website has one which covers the area around Anzac Cove at www.anzacsite.gov.au/2visiting/walk_intro.html.

Technically you don't even need a car. It is possible to get around the area using local buses and a pair of legs. TripAdvisor member 'Micool' wrote:

> You won't get the real Gallipoli experience in a tour bus. From Eceabat I caught the local bus near the ferry terminal to 'Anzac' for only 3 TL. The bus takes 20 mins and drops you at the Gabatepe museum, which features a fascinating 3D simulation of the campaign. From Gabatepe you can walk 2–3km to Anzac, following the coast-line, which is littered with many WWII-era machine-gun bunkers . . . What you want to do is walk around the entire battlefield area, a distance of about 22 km (including Hill 60.) It is exactly 11 km from Gabatepe to Chunak Bair. To get the real experience you must walk from Shrapnel Gully Cemetery near Pluggie's Plateau up Monash Valley to the terraces

behind Second Ridge, where the main Anzac defences were located. It's really tough going in dense scrub. One guy died from a heart-attack doing it in 2012[!] On the slopes I found many trenches that were once the Anzac front line. I was at Gallipoli for 8 days and it wasn't anywhere long enough to explore the whole battlefield, even though I did manage a day at Seddel Bahr where the British landed. A bus runs from near the fort at Khilid Bahr every Saturday morning. The entire peninsula is really beautiful, especially in summer. Walking also provided me with the opportunity to meet many Turks who were there sight-seeing. The only downer is that the entire battlefield is covered with thick scrub so it is hard to gain an understanding of the fields of fire. Make sure you have a swim at Anzac Cove but watch out for the fishing nets. It's easy getting back to Eceabat, as the buses run every hour. Exploring Gallipoli this way was one of the greatest adventures I have experienced.

However you travel, the most important thing, as the Australian visitor to Gallipoli reminds us, is:

But no matter what the starting point, every visitor will learn something and feel something. What is important, I think, is not the rigour of your preparation, or the seriousness with which you approach the pilgrimage. What is important is that you think enough of those who served and fought and suffered there to want to visit and see for yourself what they saw and experienced.

KEY SITES
Cemeteries
The main cemeteries are:

- Beach Cemetery at ANZAC, which Peter Hart says is 'probably the most beautiful cemetery in the world'

- Helles Memorial to the Missing
- Lone Pine Memorial and Cemetery
- Shrapnel Valley Cemetery

You can find more about them, and the other British and Anzac cemeteries on the peninsula, from the Commonwealth War Graves Commission's website: www.cwgc.org.

Museums
- Eceabat Visitors Centre, Eceabat (near Anzac Cove)
- Gallipoli War Museum, Gallipoli Historic National Park, Sahil Yolu, Gelibolu (no website, tel +90-286-566-1272)
- Kabatepe Visitors' Centre/Museum, Route 17–75, Kabatepe (www.historvius.com/kabatepe-museum-58, tel +90- 286-862-0082)
- Suvla Bay War Museum, Biyuk Anafarta (no website, telephone +90-286-834-7076)

Other Attractions
At Anzac Cove where the landings were made there is a short memorial service each day at dawn. There are some preserved trenches at Chunuk Bair. Suvla Bay is interesting, and Cape Hellas, on the tip of the peninsula, is less visited than the area around Anzac.

Further Reading
Tonie and Velmai Holt, *Major and Mrs Holt's Battlefield Guide to Gallipoli* (Pen & Sword, 1999), although somewhat dated, is still the best guide to the area. Also of interest is Nigel Steel, *Gallipoli* (Pen & Sword, 1999), which concentrates much more on the battles.

There is also an interesting description of a visit to Gallipoli on the Walking the Battlefields website at www.curme.co.uk/index.htm.

TripAdvisor has information about most of the attractions at Gallipoli with comments by visitors. There are, for example, seventy-three things to do in Gallipoli at http://www.virtualtourist.com/travel/Middle_East/Turkey/Canakkale_Ili/Galli poli-1842353/Things_To_Do-Gallipoli-TG-C-1.html#page=1&tg Count=0&themes=35. Sadly, many of the entries are rather dated.

VISITING TURKEY

Foreign Office advice for British visitors to Turkey can be found at www.gov.uk/foreign-travel-advice/turkey. The Turkish Tourism Board website at www.gototurkey.co.uk also has lots of useful information, although strangely there is nothing about visiting the battlefields.

Visitors will need a visa, which can be applied for online and costs roughly £12 (2014). Details at www.evisa.gov.tr/en.

BIBLIOGRAPHY

BOOKS

There must be several hundred books about the Gallipoli campaign and the men who fought there. The first came out within weeks of the landings, and no doubt many more will be published to coincide with the centenary. As well as editions in hardback or paperback, most of these titles are also available as e-books, ideal for taking along to the battlefields.

Pen & Sword, the publishers of this book, have produced a number of books on Gallipoli. You may find them in museum bookshops and at the excellent bookshop at The National Archives, but in general it is best to order them online at www.pen-and-sword.co.uk. And, of course, your local bookshop should be able to obtain them for you.

Gallipoli and the Dardanelles 1915–1916: Despatches from the Front (2014)
Camilla Cecil, Kira Charatan, *Under Fire in the Dardanelles* (2006)
Stephen J. Chambers, *Gully Ravine* (2002)
Stephen J. Chambers, *Anzac – The Landing* (2008)
Stephen J. Chambers, *Suvla: August Offensive – Gallipoli* (2011)
Edward Erickson, *Gallipoli: The Ottoman Campaign* (2010)
Michael Forrest, *The Defence of the Dardanelles: from Bombards to Battleships* (2012)
Major and Mrs Holt, *Major and Mrs Holt's Battlefield Guide to Gallipoli* (1999)
Nigel Steel, *Gallipoli* (1999)
Ray Westlake, *British Regiments at Gallipoli* (2004)

Here is a selection of recently published books on the campaign from other publishers:

Peter Doyle, *Battle Story: Gallipoli 1915* (Spellmount, 2011)

Philip Gariepy, *Gardens of Hell: Battles of the Gallipoli Campaign* (Potomac Publishers, 2014)

Peter Hart, *Gallipoli* (Profile Books, 2011) – the best general history of the campaign. If you only read one book, make it this one.

Robin Prior, *Gallipoli: The End of the Myth: The Final Story* (Yale University Press, 2009)

Tim Travers, *Gallipoli 1915* (Tempus, 2001)

The Gallipoli Association has a list of books about the campaign, published during the war or just after it, that can be downloaded to your Kindle or equivalent free of charge. See www.gallipoli-association.org/content/books-free-online.

There are several general histories of the war that are worth looking at if you want to put the Gallipoli campaign into context:

Peter Hart, *The Great War 1914–18* (Profile, 2014)

David Stevenson, *1914–1918: The History of the First World War* (Penguin, 2012)

Hew Strachan, *The First World War* (Simon & Schuster, 2014)

The illustrations used in this book, unless otherwise indicated, were derived from the following titles:

Ellis Ashmead-Bartlett, *The Uncensored Dardanelles* (Hutchinson, 1928)

C.E. Callwell, *The Dardanelles* (Constable, 1919)

John Masefield, *Gallipoli* (Heinemann, 1916)

Henry Nevinson, *The Dardanelles Campaign* (Nisbet, 1918)

Norman Wilkinson, *The Dardanelles* (Longman, 1916)

WEBSITES

There are numerous websites that can help your research or understanding of the campaign. These are mentioned in the appropriate place in the text. There are also some general sites that may be of interest. Wikipedia, for example, has some very good pages on the campaign. For all aspects of the British Army and its organisation Chris Baker's Long Long Trail site is superb. It also includes a section devoted to Gallipoli, with links to Sir Ian Hamilton's despatches and various e-books (www.1914-1918.net/Gallipoli.htm). The best website devoted specifically to the Gallipoli Campaign is maintained by the Gallipoli Association at www.gallipoli-association.org.

Aspects of the war at sea can be studied at the Royal Navy and Naval History Net site (www.naval-history.net), which includes material on the key naval involvement at Gallipoli.

There is also an excellent IWM website with a lot of background information based on a study tour that their staff undertook in 2000: http://archive.iwm.org.uk/upload/package/2/gallipoli/navigate.htm.

The Gallipoli Association

If you want to know more about the Gallipoli Campaign, then it is probably worth joining the Gallipoli Association, which was established in 1989 with the intention of studying the events at the Dardanelles and preserving the memory of the men who fought there. You can find out more at www.gallipoli-association.org.

INDEX